The Good Group Home
Managing for Success

by Graham Wilson

THE GOOD GROUP HOME:
MANAGING FOR SUCCESS
by Graham Wilson

Copyright ©Graham Wilson
Edited by Amelia Gilliland.
Printed in the United States of America.

ISBN 978-1-927691-12-0

ACKNOWLEDGEMENTS
I am indebted to the many people I have worked for and with. It has been a journey of unexpected richness. This book is dedicated to MAL, MS and DB for their decades of support and encouragement.

FRIDAY 501
Box 31599, Whitehorse, Yukon, Canada, Y1A 6L2
www.friday501.com, info@friday501.com

It ain't what you don't know that gets you into trouble.
It's what you know for sure that just ain't so.
Mark Twain

Several years ago I had the opportunity to observe two group homes operating in the same town but each serving a different client base. The first group home was an underfunded program that had a good reputation. A lot of the staff stayed with the organization for many years despite the relatively low pay and limited benefits. The manager motivated her team through constant coaching and the team knew they were achieving significant results with their residents. The group home hosted spectacular Halloween parties and went on regular camping trips. When their residents wanted jobs, her team grew frustrated going through government-sponsored programs and simply talked with employers directly. This led to many long-term employment opportunities for their residents. It was a happy program that achieved consistently good results.

The other program was focused on treatment and had a staff to client ratio of 1:1. The workers were paid almost twice as much as the first program, but staff morale was chronically low and staff never seemed to stay around long. Whenever I visited the program, most of the staff hid in the office while the residents watched TV or played video games. Residents told me they hated the program. They were oppositional towards staff and frequently tried to run away. The manager often blamed the poor performance of the program on the union and said he felt powerless to make changes. The program was rudderless and never seemed to achieve much.

Seeing these programs exist side by side was instructional for me. What made the difference between them? In my opinion, the difference was leadership. The manager of the first program found creative ways to motivate her staff despite her limited resources. The other program simply squandered the opportunity to do good work and never seemed to really find its legs. If you were a parent, which program would you prefer for your kid? I know which one I would choose.

It is my hope to provide some suggestions to lead any group home into a better place. I don't claim to be an expert in social services, though I have operated group homes for more than twenty-five years. When I started my career, I was surprised that there weren't any books written on group home management. I hired the most seasoned teams I could find and sought the guidance of a few successful group home managers. Gradually, I became more effective and my group homes flourished. I learned a few things along the way that have helped me manage my programs. My goal is to share some of these experiences and hopefully help other programs thrive. Through greater collaboration and motivation, a group home can become a great place to work and an even greater place for residents to live.

Many of these thoughts and opinions were learned the hard way. I often faced problems that I repeated until I learned a better way. It was this realization that motivated me to compile this project. In a way, it is also an amends to the staff and residents that I have worked with unsuccessfully. It is my hope that this book will stimulate discussion and help group home managers find their way to a better place. We have the task to provide meaningful supports to a vulnerable community of residents.

The support worker is a sleight-of-hand artist making sense out of a chaotic world to a vulnerable group of individuals. And as a result, there are few relationships more complex than managing group home staff. This book is about learning to satisfy resident and staff needs, which is a tall order. These perspectives are based on personal experiences and through discussions with many colleagues and staff. Naturally, you will be able to find many exceptions to these suggestions. You will ultimately need to work with your team to find strategies and approaches that work in your program. I have tried to avoid preaching a dogmatic truth and instead I offer these suggestions as kindly advice and hope you integrate some of the relevant ideas into your program.

Few studies have considered resident outcomes, and group homes are generally poorly understood. And even if we know the outcomes of residents, we may not know what made it work or not work for them. The reputation of group homes has been checkered and there have been many scathing critiques. As an industry, we deserve much of this criticism as many of these concerns are well founded. Poorly managed group homes are nasty places that are unsafe and disrespectful to staff, residents, and the community as a whole. Group homes are highly visible and can greatly impact a community.

Group homes tend to be thought of as the bottom of the social services food chain. Generally speaking, group home staff are not well paid and have less training than is ideal. Group homes sometimes are too busy putting out fires and, in a sense, living crisis to crisis and this limits planning and program development. When group homes function well, they can be great experiences for residents and staff alike. When a group home is working well, the staff and residents can feel like a family. Although every group home is unique, there are common qualities in successful group homes, and that is what this book is about.

1

Caring for people is an important vocation. There are many responsibilities to this work, and when done well, group homes can be great places for both staff and residents. The manager is critically important to organizing and directing staff to achieve great things. It is this responsibility that we face every day. It should motivate us to make the difficult decisions and find a balance and peace with our teams that helps them bring their "A" game. It is a challenge and a struggle, and it can be a high like no other when things are working well.

2

Support work is about designing lifestyles that work for residents. This can be physical modifications to their home but often it involves much more. It is about finding lifestyle patterns that work. By learning what their preferences are, you can adapt to them. Also, by considering their support needs and the realities in their world, you can find adaptations that work for them to achieve greater independence and fulfillment.

3

Trust your team, trust your team, trust your team. If you have done a half-decent job in recruitment and orientation, it only makes sense that you would trust them. They are your only chance to achieve meaningful results and they deserve your trust. If you learn to trust them, you will become a better manager. You will be humbled by their achievements and give them what they need to continue to get results. It all comes down to trust, and when you don't have it, your results will be severely limited.

4

Even when you try hard, you sometimes fail. That is natural. Not everything works out. But that doesn't mean you should stop trying and thinking creatively.

5

The manager and support worker relationship is usually very close. It requires honest communication and the ability from both parties to bring their best while respecting the ideas of the other. Effective teams are communicative and managers must find ways to enhance the conversation.

6

There aren't many things better than a talented team with a wealth of good support ideas. A team like this solves problems themselves and achieves consistently good results. In a way, their work seems effortless. And with success seems to come even greater success like a perpetual motion machine. Residents feel empowered and are motivated to achieve greater things and on it goes. Unfortunately, these sorts of teams are rare. But they do exist, and they are a beautiful thing.

If you're lucky enough to have a few superb staff, you can accomplish great things. Unfortunately, finding excellent staff is extraordinarily difficult. But in all honesty, I believe there are very few support workers who are given an opportunity to do good work. Create a program that nurtures creativity, professionalism, and excellence. Treat your team well and fight to keep them.

7

Sometimes staff will feel overwhelmed by the challenges of the job. Often these feelings are legitimate and understandable. The wise manager allows support workers to struggle just long enough that they find good solutions to these problems. When staff start spinning their wheels or not getting results, they likely need guidance. It isn't a good feeling to not get results and most staff will be very appreciative of any efforts to assist them.

8

Encourage strong ideas from your team and assist them to express these thoughts as clearly and powerfully as possible. This often means helping them to identify a goal and then working backwards to find ways to achieve it. The implementation is where the rubber hits the road and where a manger can be incredibly useful in helping the team state their goals.

9

Meet with your staff one-to-one regularly and help them to feel passionately about their work. Let them know that you recognize all their hard work and assure them that they are making a difference in the lives of the residents. Feeling strongly about residential care allows staff to do incredible things and overcome seemingly insurmountable obstacles.

10

When hiring, it is helpful to carefully consider

"misfits."Colorful individuals often make the best support workers, though I am uncertain why this is the case. However, they are often idealists and feel passionately about helping others reach their potential. They seem motivated by challenging situations and the ability to defy the odds. Staff like this are worth their weight in gold and it is worthwhile looking beyond superficial eccentricities to recruit staff like these.

II

I used to think that staff needed years of training and experience to become effective support workers. I now know that staff can contribute at any time in their career. In many ways, the staff with years of experience can be the most dangerous as they may be burned-out or jaded and they may hold too much responsibility in a program. Don't get me wrong: a seasoned, motivated, and skilled staff is always the best choice. However, these sorts of people are incredibly rare.

Staff new to the field trade on enthusiasm. This enthusiasm can assist with their shortfalls in other areas. And with direction and support, many deficiencies are overcome. They will make rookie mistakes and may misunderstand and exhaust management time. But these problems are usually easier to deal with than trying to encourage a burned-out staff to do their job. Group homes are powered by the energy of support workers and you can't beat an idealistic newbie in this regard.

I2

It is everyone's job to recruit new staff and everyone should consider themselves "body snatchers" in this regard. A motivated team will often refer potential staff to the manager. By encouraging the team to recruit new staff, they are empowered because they suffer the brunt of poorly recruited staff. This goes for residents too. I have hired volunteers from organizations like Special Olympics because they had a positive relationship with a resident. One of the key responsibilities of a manager is to build a capable team and having team members recommend new staff is a proven means to build strength.

13

To understand group homes, it is important to remember that initially families started them as an alternative to institutional care. These families wanted their children to live in the community in a "home-like" setting. At the time, large psychiatric hospitals and institutional care was unacceptable and was the dominant model of care for people with a range of support needs. In many places, group homes have only been around for less than fifty years. There are now thousands of group homes in North America and they are seen as a central model of social services program delivery. However, out of respect to this earlier intent it is important that we remember that group homes are seen as an alternative to institutional care and strive to create a home-like setting.

14

Not only has the growth of group homes been phenomenal, but there is also greater diversity of types of group homes. Many people still think group homes primarily cater to youths with behavioral problems; however, increasingly they support people of all ages with developmental, physical, psychiatric, behavioral, and other conditions. This diversity is a core challenge to support workers because every group home is different, and as a result the job and its goals are also widely varied. Workers must keep an open mind and embrace this diversity as a central feature of group home employment. It is common that many support workers start their careers working with youth and over time migrate to adult care. Youth work has a reputation of being highly emotionally charged and many feel it requires staff with "young legs." I have seen teams with a mean age well below 25 years.

15

Many group home managers claim they spend thirty to forty percent of their time scheduling staff. Managers tend to be the most experienced, educated, and highly paid team members. Spending such a disproportionate amount of time scheduling is a waste of resources and leads to managers feeling dissatisfied with their job. Either delegate this task to another team member or use scheduling software or outside services to free your time. Managers must be careful where they place their energy and scheduling is a time sink they need to avoid. Scheduling staff is a critical part of any organization. Poorly scheduled staff leads to excessive and expensive amounts of overtime and a disgruntled team. You can buy software that does scheduling but its usefulness is often limited. There are also services that use powerful computer systems to complete scheduling and payroll remotely. I recommend using a service that does scheduling and payroll. It can be a real money saver and keep managers where they do their best work: on the floor with their team.

16

One of the most important ways to keep detailed records is to maintain a "victory log." That is keeping a record of what works for a resident and the specifics of their successes. Not only is keeping a victory log an excellent tool for motivating staff, but it's also something that can be shared with residents and their families. When things are going well, try to figure out what is working. It's far easier to build a program based on successes rather than failures, and victory logs can be helpful with that.

17

Don't be afraid to try strategies that have worked for people with similar situations. The originality in managing group homes is often simply assembling a group of tried and true approaches. This is why it's important to keep detailed records and closely observe the work of your team.

18

"Burnout" and "support fatigue" are serious problems at most group homes. The manager that ignores this reality does so at their own peril. A single burned-out staff member can frustrate the efforts of an entire support team. Not only don't they do their work, but they also hamper the work of others. This frustrates the team and can spread like wildfire if ignored. Therefore, it is of paramount importance that managers monitor their team for signs of burnout and intervene quickly and compassionately. Sometimes outside professional counseling is required. If caught early, burnout can be treated through a variety of approaches. But left unattended, it sometimes requires the staff member to end their career as a support worker. Burnout is insidious and serious and deserves a manager's attention because it can immobilize your best staff.

19

Culling staff is not a pleasant task but is often essential to maintaining a team's morale and effectiveness. Many group homes hire untrained and uneducated staff. Not only are these staff missing a basic understanding concerning their role, but they also have not been trained to be self aware in terms of their own resiliency. As a result, even relatively minor incidents can leave them traumatized. Managers must support these staff if they are traumatized. Otherwise their careers often stall.

Some of these employees will be able to gain the necessary skills to become effective members of your team. However, others will struggle despite much orientation and training. Every manager should strive to assist every staff member to become competent; however, it usually becomes clear when new staff are poorly suited or disinterested with working in a group home environment. Under these circumstances, managers don't have any other choice than to replace staff that are not performing well.

It is crucial to help ineffective staff to move on quickly without causing too much damage. These people frustrate their co-workers but are a manager's nightmare because they can exhaust you. Not only do you have to find a way to get the work done by them, but also the slack has to be picked up by their coworkers. The resulting resentment is then redirected at the manager because the solution of simply replacing the ineffective staff is often apparent to the broader team. Firing takes time, warnings often must be given, replacement staff recruited, and other matters can bog down a manager's workday. But it's important to move swiftly with the knowledge that the program will ultimately benefit the short-term dislocation.

20

Managers should strive to maintain an environment of professionalism and not be paralyzed by a staff member's personal issues. In these cases, it is often enough to meet with the staff and discuss their performance issues and areas for improvement immediately. Capable staff are often aware of these problems and have enough insight to make the necessary adjustments and improve their performance. However, just as often they tend to minimize and deny any issues. If the manager has access to any empirical data that is irrefutable, it is important to allow this information to lead the conversation.

21

Staff need to believe in their residents potential and be motivated to make a positive difference in their lives. Attitude is hugely important throughout ones career. Attitude doesn't matter much if you work on an assembly line; however, when you work in social services a positive perspective is essential. As a result, managers must hire for attitude rather than skills alone. Staff can relatively easily learn skills but attitude is much more challenging. When interviewing prospective staff, try to determine whether they embrace concepts like dignity of choice by residents or even the benefits of normalization. A good attitude can help even the weakest staff achieve great results.

22

Staff must show compassion at all times – this is a central promise of care. Residents must never feel judged or diminished in any way. This trust is essential for residents to develop skills and grow. We must stop short of calling it love, but it needs to be unconditional care. When we provide this environment, residents have the conditions to grow over time. This requires a lot of awareness by the manager and the care team as a whole.

23

In the minds of many residents, caregivers are considered "oppressors." Caregivers may include teachers, principles, scoutmasters, group home staff, or others. In the resident's life caregivers may have exerted control and have dealt with them without compassion. This is a reality for many residents. It is important for group homes to reach these residents by developing a relationship of trust and compassion. Until this relationship is formed, staff will be thought of as oppressors and there will always be distrust and dishonesty. Always avoid being skeptical or critical with residents and never force them to live "small" lives.

24

Most support workers are extremely kind people. However, many need to be encouraged to be kind to themselves. Support work can be challenging and can lead to health problems, psychological problems, emotional problems and/or substance abuse. Therefore, it's important for managers to encourage their staff to take care of themselves and be kind to themselves. Benefit packages can encourage this practice. After difficult shifts, a gift of a massage or a pass to the pool can do wonders to encourage self care.

25

When staff are controlling their own personal triggers, they become mindful. There are two types of memory. The first type of memory is recall, which is what most people consider to be memory. The second type of memory is called explicit memory and is the way we record emotions. By understanding that there are different ways we recall periods of our life, we can provide more mindful care.

26

One of the realities that isn't discussed often is that many group home staff were raised in dysfunctional homes. This is a reality that is common throughout social services and explains many common behavior problems. These staff tend to develop unhealthy relationships at work and need close supervision and support. Their personal experiences can be beneficial to relating to residents but these staff deserve a manager's attention.

27

Staff perform best when they feel supported. Managers must be aware of this reality and offer clarity and support to the team on a continuous basis. This requires managers to be somewhat aware of the personal goals and needs of each staff member. The work environment needs to be flexible to the needs of staff. However, this is often a challenging line to tow because it is easy to fall into dependent relationships with staff. Through experience, managers gain an ability to discern staff who are experiencing infrequent crisis with those with turbulent lives. Staff that are chronically in personal crisis are poorly suited to work in group homes and must be encouraged to find more suitable employment. This includes staff suffering from conditions such as addiction or chronic depression.

28

In many small programs, managers frequently work with residents as well as administering the program. This is especially true when programs are short staffed or small in scale. This is an opportunity for managers to "strut their stuff" and role model effective strategies. A team that knows their manager has mastered many of the elements of their job has greater respect for the manager. Role modeling is a powerful instructive tool and can whittle down the most complex care plan to its essence. This is why virtually all the best group home managers I have met have mastered the skills of support workers and have many years of front-line experience.

29

A group home can be the hub in a resident's life. However, it is just one piece of the puzzle and a person still needs education, employment, recreation, and a variety of other opportunities to live a full life. Therefore, it's important for the group home manager to be an advocate to develop these other aspects of a person's life. Often the group home is the central resource for a person and other services will often defer to your opinion. In preparation, it's important to ask the resident what they want and to strategize with them.

30

When you're encouraging your team to take risks, you

must make them feel as secure as possible. The key question is what happens when a staff member fails. If an organization considers failure a negative performance issue the team will be unlikely to be risk takers. Therefore, it is important for managers to support staff as much when they fail as when they succeed. Managers in these instances should never be seen as punitive but rather as partners in the team's ups and downs.

31

Encourage staff and residents to swing for the fences. It's okay to not always be successful but there is something wrong with not trying. As trite as this sounds, it's important for people to dream big and have ambitious goals.

32

If your team has creativity, intuition, and trust you will be well on your way to having a good group home. There isn't one single way to achieve these qualities, but when they are present you will know it and your residents will prosper. When things are going well, try to figure out why and build on those qualities and encourage your team to continue to develop fresh and innovative approaches. Find unconventional ways to engage the team in conversations - something as simple as going for a walk can encourage a more effective conversation. In some ways it's best to become even more supportive during times of success and to be observant as to what's working and why.

33

Managers need to be passionate about their group homes. You can't phone it in. You must believe that your residents can achieve incredible things and your team can help them reach their goals. You want to motivate your team and challenge them to deliver the best supports you can imagine. Unfortunately, short-term goals tend to get the most attention. Make sure your team also considers the resident's long term goals and that the short-term goals are addressing where the person wants their life to lead.

34

Sleep is one of the most important aspects of care. The relationship between behavior and sleep is obvious – ask anybody with overtired toddlers. Therefore, it is important to encourage residents and staff to get more than six hours of sleep each night. This requires close monitoring and may require a deliberate routine to slowly wind down the day by dimming lights and lowering the volume of stereos or TVs to queue residents that sleep is imminent. If residents are routinely having difficulty sleeping, consultation with family doctors or other supports may be required. For some people, getting enough sleep can be very challenging and will require planning and support to establish routines that help them rest.

35

There are certain employment realities that a manager can't change. Firstly, support workers tend to be underpaid when compared to other industries. Support work can also be dangerous, particularly in the case of mental health and youth workers. These are realities that you can often improve but can't usually correct one-hundred percent. Therefore, it is important that managers acknowledge these realities and be grateful to their employees for continuing care despite these liabilities.

36

Support workers can become traumatized or exhausted in crisis-prone group homes. Under these conditions, it's easy to fall into dysfunctional relationships with residents. In these group homes, staff are often expected to "wing it"and there isn't a well-defined care model with clearly defined roles and responsibilities. Managers can also be impacted by frequent and intense crisis. Managers preoccupied with day-to-day survival rather than long-term strategic planning rarely succeed. When programs experience frequent crisis, changes need to be made swiftly to reduce the frequency and intensity of future crisis.

37

Caring for people is a partnership amongst many people, including health professionals, funding agencies, families, residents, and the community. However, you have to work on the structure of collaboration. Will you schedule weekly meetings? Will you exchange all personal information to everyone? Who will make the final decision? I've found that there isn't a single, one-size-fits-all solution. The key is to keep the dialog flowing.

38

Managers need to be selective about which projects will benefit from collaboration. Not everything needs to be discussed by the team. Long meetings with lots of detail are boring and are rarely effective. It's important to give priority to the most important issues and to do so in thumbnail detail. Group homes aren't a democracy but rather run by leaders who consult and make informed, reasonable decisions.

39

Technologies like computer databases are an excellent tool for tracking care and encouraging collaboration. Caregivers can see what other staff are doing, collaborate, and brag about successes. By creating an atmosphere of collaboration, the manager often minimizes their conflict with support workers and can assume the role of traffic cop or cheerleader, which is highly desirable.

40

Managers should never have angry outbursts. It's unprofessional, counterproductive, and role models unacceptable workplace behavior. Remember the adage "When angry, you'll make the best speech you'll ever regret."Therefore, always keep your emotions in check. When you feel your temper rise, take a walk or do whatever you need to calm down and collect your thoughts and emotions.

41

The management style of group homes should strive to be a network rather than a hierarchy. Hierarchies are cumbersome and ineffective in group homes. Many managers are command-and-control and top-down, and as a result need to work twenty hours a day. This makes sense since it is often the type of management we received when we started out. And since most managers have limited management training, they struggle. However, a team that collaborates and establishes healthy boundaries and roles don't require traditional management. Hierarchical leadership doesn't scale well and leads to adversarial relationships with support workers and should be avoided at all costs.

42

The easiest way to improve care is to involve residents and their families in decision making whenever possible or practical. This is more than simply calling them quarterly for obligatory meetings. Pull them in close and make them feel listened to. What are the resident's long-term goals? What are the expectations of the group home? What is the caregiving team missing? Consultation should be ongoing and frequent. Most of the best discussions will be informal and on the fly.

43

Size matters, and it's easiest to work in small support teams. Many managers don't have the training or support to run large operations. Small group homes are inherently more personal and less unwieldy and tend to be easier to manage and lead. Plus, when mistakes or setbacks occur, they tend to be easier to recover from. Group homes tend to function best when residents live together in small numbers. Often large group homes feel like mini institutions and can feel cold and impersonal. Large groupings can be chaotic and residents can become over-stimulated or display stress behaviors.

44

When you get the culture right in a group home, great things happen. It takes a charismatic manager who can motivate and challenge their team to achieve great outcomes with their residents. Therefore, knowing what to praise takes judgement. Personally, I think it's better to limit praise to just the exceptional things rather than praising everything.

45

Adopt ways to effectively evaluate your staff. Unless your staff are getting reasonable results with the residents, changes need to be made. Working with your residents is a privilege. You want to have the highest effectiveness and compensate as well as possible. You want to recognize and reward your best support workers. You can't have a good group home without good support workers. If your group home is under performing, do what it takes to get the wheels on the bus.

46

When going to doctor appointments always collect a resident's medications and bring them to the appointment. Have the doctor check the medications to ensure they are correct. It is surprising how frequent medication mistakes are made at doctor's offices and pharmacies.

47

Managers should be brutally honest about their strengths and weaknesses. Many of the things you struggle with are things that will always challenge you. After all, nobody is good at everything. Therefore, it's necessary to find people who can help with the tasks that you feel are personally difficult or onerous. For instance, I knew that bookkeeping is something that I've never been interested in or had much aptitude for. But when I was starting out, I found a wonderful bookkeeper who understood the needs of my group home. As a result, for the past twenty-five years my group homes have had organized financial statements and records that most businesses would envy. The expense of hiring a bookkeeper has saved me a great deal of money and worry. I have been able to make informed financial decisions and have avoided a world of hurt.

When contracting out parts of your job, you should find other areas to focus your skills and interests. The time saved by hiring someone to schedule your staff can be better spent consulting with families or professionals involved in the program's care. This strategy will help you avoid burnout and will increase your job satisfaction and your performance. The key is to accurately appraise your skills and interests and focus on areas where you can make the greatest positive impacts.

48

Because of the nature of group home budgets, there is a limited ability to reduce costs year to year. But group homes must generate a profit to grow and remain viable. The deprecation of capital costs such as furniture, equipment, and vehicles is usually relatively minor. Resist the urge to reduce costs by trying to reduce staffing costs, as the long-term impacts to your program can be huge.

49

Do the hard part of your job. Many group home managers stay busy with the easier-to-accomplish tasks. Many managers have told me that they find the hardest task is to work with staff. Trying to motivate and orient a team to consistently provide good service can be daunting and should be the highest priority to managers. The easiest tasks are easier to delegate and you can hire people to accomplish them. Don't ignore the hard tasks.

50

There is a saying that the best fertilizer is a gardener's footprints. With a healthy team, a manager needs to frequent their program. Not always in a formal way, but in frequent and unexpected ways. A manager can stop by for a coffee or a meal and visit with residents and staff. Managers can also offer to help with outings or help hang a bird house with residents, clean a vehicle, or go out for ice cream. These efforts show a willingness to pitch in and an understanding of the importance of the smaller moments.

51

You want to keep good records so that you can communicate with future support workers. If you keep a record of what you're trying with an individual and how it's working, you are forming a commitment. You are reaching out to those caregivers with the generosity of having them understand what you did and how you did it.

52

If you don't know what your resident wants, it's very unlikely you'll be able to give them care that makes sense to them. Many of your efforts will either fail or only partly succeed. By knowing what they want, you are better able to plan for success and ensure their lives are as fulfilled as possible.

53

When no conceivable good can come from a conflict, don't engage.

54

Often in discussions with staff and residents, great truths will be revealed. Sometimes these things happen in throwaway moments when you're doing other things like driving in a car or buying groceries.

55

You shouldn't assume that through coaching, staff will become better at their jobs. Sometimes regardless of the effort that is made they will never be very good support workers. In these cases, carefully offer your insight and help them move onto other employment.

56

A manager must be highly organized and always follow through. A manager must not get distracted and persevere until the task is completed. If a manager isn't able to complete things, they will be ineffectual.

57

A team is just a group of people. An effective manager must be a good listener and have an ability to motivate the team. The manager must be able to guide the team and praise and encourage them to keep trying.

58

Sometimes it is necessary to change banks. If your bank doesn't support your business's goals or needs, you should begin shopping around for a better fit. This isn't always easy and often can be a little scary, but if it's necessary you really don't have a choice. For this reason, it's important to have up-to-date financial statements at all times. It is also important to have financial statements from all previous years so that you can clearly show how your business has performed. If you have had financial difficulties, be prepared to explain what happened and make sure to stress how you overcame these challenges. Bank managers are good at spotting lies, so make sure you tell the truth. Every business goes through ups and downs, and if you show how you acknowledged a problem and modified your course, you gain credibility.

59

Don't hesitate to delegate from the very start of your business. It will develop your team's abilities to perform a wider range of tasks. Plus, as you prepare to retire or concentrate on other aspects of your business, you will be easy to replace.

60

A manager needs to decide to make their group home the best it can be. Understand that it is a decision to develop a good group home and do whatever is needed to improve your program. It all starts with committing to excellence and that is a decision.

61

Make sure not to undervalue the importance and value of your work. An effective manager is worth their weight in gold, and if you're getting results, your team and residents will notice. Make sure you pay yourself well and reward your abilities whenever possible. It's very common for managers to undervalue their work and this leads to problems.

62

When contracting people to do work for you, it's important to be specific and task oriented. For this reason it's helpful to always have written work orders with tradesmen and consultants. Don't be afraid to outline the nature of the work in detail, the time you envision the work to be complete, and its cost. Any ambiguity is your fault and it's critical to convey expectations as clearly and detailed as possible.

63

If you micromanage staff, the best ones leave. And if the best ones leave, the ones you have left require more micromanagement. Pretty soon, you feel like you are running a police state. You end up with below-average employees in terms of motivation and ability, and your work week expands from 40 hours a week to twenty-four/seven. These sorts of teams become addicted to close direction; if they aren't told to do something, it will never get done. These teams under perform and will frustrate residents and management efforts. Often it is best to state a goal and let the team decide (with guidance) how to reach that goal.

64

Many group homes fall into the trap of being custodial. Activities and programs are delivered to a group and are not specifically tailored to any one individual. The easiest way to avoid being custodial is to embrace person-centered planning from the start. When you're person centered, surprising opportunities arise.

65

Hold regular "house meetings" to establish house rules and goals and air any grievances. It is expected that certain standards of care be established in all group homes. Residents must be informed of these standards when they move in and be reminded of house rules from time to time. Sometimes a written contract or posted house rules work well, though you don't want the house to feel institutional.

66

House meetings can explore these rules and standards and hopefully make changes when necessary. Staff or residents should take notes and make sure residents feel listened to and empowered. As residents gain skills in speaking their minds, the group home can better adapt to what they envision it needs to be. Residents need to know that they can set many standards of care and that the role of the support worker is not to oppress them. Trusted family members can help explain standards or expectations to residents if necessary.

67

Encourage funding agencies, social workers, and family doctors to regularly visit the group home to help them understand the service and build a rapport. This is often most effective when things are going well and you can stress the goals of the program. When things are not going well, the broader team will remember the way things usually work and assist you in getting back to "normal." This is more than public relations, as many of these people can provide valuable support and insight.

68

Smaller groupings tend to foster peacefulness and acceptance by the community. You are trying to build a home. A home can be many things, but perhaps most importantly a sanctuary from the chaos of the world.

69

Decision making should not be based on rank, and the best idea in the room must always win. Therefore, effective managers must solicit opinions and ideas from all corners of the team without judgment or hesitation. The ultimate decision does not have to be a consensus. It just has to be the idea with the best chance of success. By democratizing decision making, the team is empowered and better able to resolve problems with greater independence.

70

When you help a resident become more independent or happier or fulfilled, you not only help that person, but you also help their friends and family. When the resident is doing well, their entire support network notices and warms-up to your program and other opportunities tend to emerge.

71

We often form opinions based on superficial ideas or an

incomplete understanding of what is in front of us. For this reason, it's important to understand that our opinions need to shift if new information comes to light. If you're well intentioned and working collaboratively with others, changing your mind won't be seen as a weakness.

72

Give credit where credit is due. Don't take credit for some-body else's ideas or work. Just the simple act of giving credit and being genuinely grateful will build the respect of your team.

73

Group homes tend to be emotionally messy places. People's passions tend to merge and the outcome can be somewhat unpredictable and often heightened. I tend to love this energy and find it interesting to try to navigate waters that are far from calm. But it is important staff try not to be too controlling as this only leads to frustration and burnout. Accepting the reality that group homes are emotionally messy allows staff to better understand their role and adjust their expectations.

74

It's important to remember that your family must always be a priority. I am sometimes saddened to hear group home managers moan about how little time they take off for fam-ily vacations or important things like maternity/paternity leave. Therefore, I suggest group home managers lead by example and take care of their families by taking signifi-cant leave. This will encourage the rest of the team to take off similar leaves for their families. In the long run, encouraging staff to be connected with their families will pay off. The team will be happier, better balanced, and more resilient in coping with stress at work.

75

Having low expectations can rob a resident of their independence and their potential to live a fulfilling life. It is well proven that having positive expectations can help a person succeed and grow. However, it's surprising how many support workers believe their residents are incapable and dependent on paid professionals to provide a wide range of support services. For a support worker to be successful, they need to believe in the potential of their residents and carefully provide assistance only when absolutely necessary.

76

Sometimes managers are reluctant to ask for the opinions of others. I'm not sure why this is the case, but it is very common. Having other managers on your speed dial can really help get your team organized. Several times, especially when I was inexperienced, their suggestions helped me shape supports and avoid pitfalls. Sometimes it's just healthy to complain about persistent, seemingly unsolvable problems and get specific advice from someone you trust. I strongly recommend managers carefully consider supports from others in the industry that can help guide them. The opinions you receive can sometimes make or break your business and avoiding pitfalls is the name of the game.

77

You want to create an environment where support workers can do their best work. You want the business to fade into the background and you want to help your team achieve their goals in any way necessary.

78

Accept that it is not possible to get everything done at a group home. Things will always be incomplete and that is okay.

79

Avoiding getting sued can lead to making conservative and ineffective decisions. Mostly, people sue when they are hurt or angry, and it's important to always be clear about expectations. It's important for all agreements to be written clearly in plain English so that both parties know what they are agreeing to. If both parties know what they are agreeing to, they are much less likely to feel hurt and angry because they know what they signed.

80

Managers tend to either spend a lot of money with lawyers to draft lengthy and complex agreements or they download templates that are wordy and oftentimes unspecific to the group home business. Instead of drafting lengthy agreements, consider just adding a clause making each party agree to binding informal arbitration in case of a dispute. In essence, both parties pick a lawyer and the two lawyers pick a third lawyer. The third lawyer then spends a few hours looking at memos, emails, and briefs and decides who is right. This dispute mechanism works because both sides realize they can't outspend the other side to win the dispute. In total, this resolution will cost less than a couple of thousand dollars and be settled relatively quickly. It prevents the resolution from spinning out of control in terms of cost and bullying tactics. And it's great to already have a fair and straightforward means to resolve things.

81

Profit is not the point in managing group homes. Sure, you don't want to run a program into the red, but forget about trying to generate big profits. Instead, consider broader social concerns like value, purpose, and sustainability.

82

Always be honest with your staff and residents and never buffer them from the consequences of their actions. Don't be scared to share hard truths at a time and in a way that is supportive and compassionate.

83

In many regions funding agencies encourage mediocrity and are risk adverse. They shroud residents in poorly trained and unsupported staff who make well-intentioned but ultimately ineffective caregivers. To make an impact, we must encourage our teams to let residents live with minimal intervention so their independence isn't harmed. The goal is to be clear about boundaries and to always encourage residents to live full lives that may be imperfect and challenging but are rich and fulfilling.

84

Managers must sometimes go contrary to the system and the status quo. There are inherent risks but ultimately bureaucratic systems are often destructive and harmful to residents. The stakes are too high to simply provide support systems that are out dated and not progressive. In this instance, managers must consider themselves as guerrilla caregivers and go above and beyond what is sanctioned and expected.

85

A good manager is often part salesman as they have to sometimes sell a support team, residents, families, and social workers on a strategy. The best plans are often creative and fun, and it's important to breathe freshness into a support plan. This is always easy but almost always yields the most success.

It's all about saying the right thing in the right way. This isn't easy, but when it's done well the broader team will be happier and more successful. The best managers will be able to reduce a sophisticated plan of care or a support strategy into the fewest words.

86

Basically you want to encourage your residents to feel they have a long life and you are there to help them get what they want. This may seem really broad and vague but it reflects what is ahead of you as a manager. It is the promise of your care and should be the mantra of your team.

87

Some managers cater to government agencies and social workers. They don't always believe in the right things. You want to foster a rebel spirit and fight for the best care for your residents and the needs of your staff.

88

It's a beautiful thing to walk into a good group home. Residents and staff are active and engaged in their community. There is an energy that is indescribable but palpable. They have an energy and enthusiasm that helps residents reach their dreams. It is a huge responsibility but being a manager of a good group home is one of life's greatest pleasures.

89

Sometimes in negotiations it's important to take a stand on a minor issue. This usually feels like posturing but it allows the other side to get a glimpse that you're not a pushover and will take a stand when necessary.

90

There are lots of ways to address workplace wellness. Reducing stress and increasing cooperation and collaboration is the ultimate goal. Having a benefits package that broadly meets the goals of wellness is a start. Being able to encourage staff to take yoga by subsidizing is a good start. Paying for gym memberships or massages is an effective way to support your team.

91

Unless you work with children, assume the resident is in charge. This is difficult for old-school caregivers to accept and much training and reorientation may be necessary for these individuals. Quite simply, it's important to ask whose life it is.

92

Support workers must sublimate their feelings, respect boundaries, and assume residents can make good decisions with appropriate support. This is often a sticky situation and residents should have the opportunity to experience the consequences of their actions. However, support workers need to intervene when they feel these consequences will be too destructive and counterproductive.

93

It is essential for boundaries to be established as principles of care for all group homes. Some of these standards are set externally, such as accounting practices, contract specific issues, and the like. But residents and staff can establish many standards internally.

94

The role of the support worker is to lead, not control, and this relationship is built on trust. When support workers exert power and control, residents tend to see them as compassionate fascists

95

Support work is very personal, and over time support workers develop complex relationships with residents. Once a relationship has matured and there is rapport, great things can be accomplished. The goal is to deepen relationships and live a happy life.

Just as support workers and residents require a good rapport, managers and support workers also require a good rapport. This level of communication allows great things to be accomplished and is satisfying for everyone involved.

96

A climate of trust must be felt by family and the support team. Once trust has been established, results will soon follow. By being honest, frank, and kind, residents learn to trust. Trust is often a difficult thing to achieve and can take an enormous amount of time.

97

For residents that have been traumatized, their behaviors may appear to derail good efforts. In these cases, trauma has to be central in all planning. Most group homes need to better understand trauma and become trauma-based in the delivery of services.

98

Sometimes staff are traumatized while at work. I have seen relatively minor incidents that have left staff thoroughly traumatized. Once the incident is over and everyone is safe, it is important that mangers check the well being of their staff. Having the staff describe the critical incident in detail is a valuable way for them to establish in their minds what really happened. If this intervention doesn't happen, staff are prone to fabricate and distort the incident in their minds eye. At that point, it may be best to have a trained counsellor debrief the traumatized staff. Customarily, I offer counselling with a psychologist with knowledge of my program followed by a massage or other bodywork. I can attest to a much better outcome as a result.

99

All teams are short on time and require concise, clear direction and plans. Staff should be encouraged to spend the first fifteen minutes of each day planning how to spend their time. I'm a convert to the world of "to-do" lists after years of fighting their unquestioned usefulness. It's shocking how many disorganized and inefficient staff there are. With coaching, there can be dramatic performance improvements.

100

There are lots of interesting ideas out there. The challenge is to develop a plan of care that is simple and elegant. Use language that fosters action and have systems that ensure follow-up. Therefore, after-action reviews are essential. The team needs to study, discuss, and think constantly.

101

Simple ideas tend to be easier to execute and implement and often solve complex problems. Often staff try to implement strategies that are too complex with too many steps.

Try to break down these big ideas into smaller ideas and smaller steps.

102

What is the promise of the care from the resident's perspective? Generally it is best to meet present needs rather than future ones.

103

Strategy counts but often the best support workers are opportunists rather than strategists. For this reason, some programs keep success journals, which are records of strategies that have worked.

104

Don't hesitate to make changes or modifications on the fly. Consider the example from the US automobile industry. For decades Detroit knew that people wanted safer, more reliable, and economical cars and did little to meet this demand. The Japanese auto manufactures capitalized on this opportunity and soon eclipsed US auto sales. The goal is to act quickly once you know what needs to be corrected. By being more immediate, your program will remain relevant and better able to cope with both crisis and opportunity.

105

Some of the things you reach for, you and your residents shouldn't get. It's very human to have some big, lofty hopes even if they are somewhat unrealistic.

106

Working with people is hard work. Helping them reach goals is even harder. Change and growth are difficult to measure. The best goals are small, attainable, and measurable. Baby steps also foster less fear, resistance, and mistrust by residents.

107

Avoid allowing residents to make self-destructive choices that don't promote personal growth or are damaging to others. Support workers should avoid saying "it's their choice" when a resident is making self-destructive choices and intervene as unobtrusively as possible.

108

The mantra for support workers should be "all behavior is purposeful." There is always a reason for a behavior, and what may appear as a symptom is likely an adaptation. This can be difficult to understand, especially at times of crisis. The prudent question support workers should ask is "What happened to you?" not "What's wrong with you?" Ultimately, behavior is language, and it's important to try to figure out what a behavior is saying.

109

Most group homes adopt custodial models of care, and this is unfortunate. These group homes tend to be inefficient and have lower staff and resident fulfillment. But there is an alternative: the person-centered group home. Generally speaking, these homes tend to have only two or three people living together. Person-centered group homes tend to have much better resident outcomes. These teams aren't better paid but almost always have better morale and staff retention. These teams are more creative and flexible and staff feel empowered.

110

Group homes need to develop an internal care community within their organization. They also need to link with schools, vocational opportunities, recreation programs, etc. Fortunately, in many jurisdictions generic resources are underused and it is relatively easy to accommodate special needs.

The goal is to develop a cluster of services outside of paid residential staff. Many residents have staff but not support networks, and while this pursuit can be challenging it is always worthwhile. Inclusion is extremely important and should be pursued vigorously by a care team. Residents shouldn't have all their eggs in one program's basket.

111

Every resident needs a "champion." A champion is a team member who advocates for a particular resident. Basically, it is someone who feels strongly about the resident's abilities and needs and is willing to advocate for them. In many group homes this person is called a key worker. The key worker should be willing to establish strong ties with a resident's family and significant supports, such as employers or teachers. The role of the key worker then becomes a bridge to bring any concerns or suggestions to the broader team. The key worker coordinates a resident's supports and ensures their needs are being met.

112

Culture is one of the most critical considerations in any plan of care, and unfortunately it is often overlooked. Culture includes religion, language, food, music, and other things. It can also include gender and age.

To best understand and adapt to this cultural context, the support team should be culturally integrated and ideally include members of a resident's community. Cross-cultural sensitivity can express itself in many tangible and intangible ways and support workers should always be aware that cultural expression can happen in surprising, unpredictable ways. The group home needs to consult with cultural leaders as much as possible and be willing to adapt and accommodate.

113

Great support workers are not necessarily geniuses or highly educated but are always great listeners. Their goal is to establish a conversation with residents rather than a monologue. They encourage residents to make good choices and participate in a well-rounded life. They respond to residents quickly and with compassion and understanding. Great things happen when a resident feels they are being heard.

114

Support workers must be accessible to residents and be willing to listen to anything and act promptly – this must be an implicit understanding with the resident. Likewise, managers must also be immediately available to staff to help resolve problems and give guidance.

115

There is no substitute for really knowing your residents and this often takes a lot of time and effort. Developing this rapport often reveals lots of surprises. Once you get to know your staff and residents, you can often anticipate outcomes. When you learn what residents like and don't like, your job shifts to helping them set goals to get what they want. If you don't know your residents, you will never be able to effectively help them because you won't know what they want out of life. It is only when we know what a resident wants that we can direct care. Without direction, the world can be random, hopeless, and frustrating.

116

Through experience, most support workers learn to predict resident behaviors. For many residents, the best predictor of future behavior is past behavior. Experienced support workers understand this reality and have the ability to predict reliably. These predictions can be extremely valuable in day-to-day programming.

117

In group homes we often deal with inappropriate behaviors that are learned. Learned behaviors are frequently attention seeking and can be challenging to deal with. Support workers should try to understand the root cause of the behavior and treat it as a symptom of something potentially larger. Staff should try to help residents change behaviors to more normalized, less problematic behaviors. This often involves "unlearning" behaviors and attitudes and can be difficult and scary for residents and support workers alike. Doing this well can greatly enhance the residents well being and can be a metaphor for more generalized growth and development.

118

Encourage staff to establish unique relationships with residents. Residents are individuals and shouldn't be treated collectively or impersonally. Residents should feel they really matter and their personalities are appreciated. Support work by its very nature is deeply personal for residents and staff and this reality is crucially important.

119

To impact on a resident's life, support workers must strive to make each and every day count. In group homes the adage "what have you done for me lately?" is extremely relevant.

120

By being inventive and creative, problems get solved. Good enough is never good enough when you are working with people. Therefore, keep reinventing your program. Staying the same is a huge risk.

121

It usually doesn't take much to get a good idea off the ground in successful group homes. Support workers must strive to reduce the time from idea to execution. It may help to consider this as the "idea cycle time" and the shorter the time from idea to execution is almost always better. Innovation is a group activity and should include the entire team as well as residents.

122

Most experienced support workers carry a huge insight and intuition, which is often accurate and unbelievably valuable. Sometimes following your gut is your best option when making choices.

123

There are many unpredictable support opportunities in group homes, and at the end of the day we often don't know why a particular strategy works or doesn't work. This is one of the great ironies of residential work, and it is perilous to assume a support team has all the answers. Embrace the fact that sometimes we do not understand why something works. Take credit for the success – you probably deserve the praise.

124

Support work often requires on-the-spot decision making and this usually happens while doing many things at the same time. Therefore, decide now and analyze later, and realize that change hurts but indecision kills.

125

What is a mistake? How does your group home define failure? Sometimes it is more useful to think of mistakes as learning experiences rather than mistakes. As the adage goes, "nothing ventured, nothing gained."

In group homes not taking enough risk is very dangerous and it is important to fail within parameters.

Allowing residents to make mistakes is also important,

as trial and error is the way we learn many things. It is usually better to try something than to do nothing. However, an important diagnostic question is "what happens when staff and/or residents fail?" Learn from mistakes and understand that there is no doing without mistakes, setbacks, and dead-ends.

126

It is critical to perform post mortems on mistakes and to adequately debrief all staff. In effective group homes, staff success and failure is often rewarded equally. However, there is a difference between smart mistakes and dumb mistakes. Staff tend to make more dumb mistakes when they are tired, alone, or unsure.

127

Develop a tradition of responsible risk taking in order to help the resident succeed. By planning to take risks and making mistakes, we unhitch from achieving "success" all the time. Caregivers must expect setbacks and concentrate on bouncing back when things don't work out as planned. After all, it's what we do with life's knocks that really counts.

128

Support workers must understand how the business works and concentrate on being fiscally lean and mean. In a very real sense you want to apply guerrilla tactics because money is precious. Buy what you need and don't spend a cent more. All group homes must strive to be financially healthy as this is in everyone's best interest. By avoiding debt, unnecessary growth, and being flexible and adaptable to resident needs, a group home remains relevant.

Group homes must be financially accountable and maintain good, up-to-date financial records. Bookkeeping should be done using computers so that all payroll and expense information is immediately retrievable by managers. All group homes are expensive to operate and run and require careful financial planning and collaboration. Managers must find ways to pay staff well and develop non-monetary means to reward as well. For instance, offering flexible work hours can be a management hassle but the benefit to support workers can be enormous. These measures will be deeply valued by the team and lead to improved morale.

One of the core realities is that group homes are directly accountable to funding agencies and government review. While this sounds reasonable, it can lead to a general malaise of the group home. Group homes are responsible to outside agencies but their primary responsibility is to the resident. Government expectations and standards are often ridiculously low. Governments encourage group homes to aim low and often place obstacles and objections in front of creative, flexible programs. Group homes must show funding and oversight agencies that much more is possible, and that there is a better way.

129

Support workers should have access to contractual standards of care and related material. This will help them understand the expectations of various government agencies, funding, and oversight bodies.

130

The benefit of using IT in group homes is enormous. Not only does it reduce operational costs, but it can also increase collaboration and team performance. Computers and database systems can streamline work and give immediate access to important data and reports. However, these systems can distract staff and occupy their time with irrelevant report writing. The core of any appropriate database system is its ability to record and retrieve only what is important or necessary. In group homes, need to know must always beat nice to know. Time and energy are too precious to waste on the nonessential.

131

I noticed a while ago that if you graphed the first few years of financial costs associated with a resident that it resembled a hockey stick. It has been my experience that in a resident's first six months of care, there is a net financial loss due to the establishment of routines and programs. After six months to a year, the program breaks even financially as the program delivers services more efficiently and predictably. The second year of care recovers the costs incurred in the first six months and by the third year care is established and able to support itself.

132

Group homes should try to specialize and develop a niche – this can be either by resident age, disability, or other characteristics. When a group home has success with a certain type of resident, they should seek future residents with similar attributes or needs. Eventually, the group home will become known as being "specialists" and this has value and worth.

133

Sometimes group homes need to be closed. Frequently this is because the team has lost energy, direction, and hope. Often, only a few key people will drive a group home and when these people lose their way or leave a group homes' survival is in doubt. For this reason, it is sometimes best for a group home to close and a new group home with fresh ideas, energy, and perspectives to be developed. At the time this is often painful to understand but in the course of time it is usually beneficial for the residents to relocate to a new resource.

134

Every group home needs short procedure manuals and clear philosophy statements. These statements help the broader team understand the group home's goals and how energy is being allocated. Look around at other programs, adjust yourself accordingly, and avoid reinventing the wheel. These manuals must be easy to access and preferably online so staff can refer to them frequently.

135

A support worker's goals are to create an environment that works, develop a support environment that organizes, and develop a support environment that is meaningful and fun.

136

Support workers should shield residents from bureaucrats.

When bureaucrats enter a resident's life, they often are destructive and disappointing. Front-line staff can also be damaged by bureaucrats. Staff should also be buffered from negativity and criticism from outsiders. The problem with bureaucrats is that they often wield significant power and are more concerned with the law and less concerned with what is effective or ethical.

Managers must appreciate that even the most burned-out, running-out-the-clock-so-they-can-cash-in-their-government-pension bureaucrat has something to offer. You just may not want them to interfere with your front-line team.

137

A rescuer sees residents as being helpless or hopeless. A rescuer assumes a burden of helping – this burden often continues to increase until the support worker is overwhelmed or fatigued. In the end, the support worker feels powerless and victimized. A support worker is rescuing when they do something for a resident that the resident can do for themselves. When you rescue, you create dependency and promote powerlessness. As Claude Steiner has written: "Every situation in which one person needs help from another is potentially also a situation in which one person can become a Rescuer and another person can become a Victim. The role of Rescuer is a role in which one person, in a one-up position, denies to or diminishes in another person, the Victim, the power of helping herself by accepting a request for help without making demands for equal participation, by imposing help without a request for it, or by helping when one doesn't really want to help."

Rescuing is an easy trap for support workers to find themselves in with residents. It almost always leads to resident over-dependence, support worker burnout, and other negative feelings such as guilt or resentment. Therefore, avoid rescuing at all costs.

138

Residents must be encouraged to see they have choices in their lives. And they must be encouraged to live with as much independence as possible. It is healthy and leads to many beneficial outcomes.

139

What is a good life? People with disabilities or behavioral problems have the same capacity to enjoy life and to be fulfilled. The gap between potential and reality can lead to dissatisfaction and a lack of fulfillment. Support workers mustn't ignore a resident's deepest purposes. Life is fulfilling when one has passions and interests. Support workers aren't trying to make life "easy" and their role is to help residents to achieve things that are important to them. Residents need something to look forward to and life needs to make sense. Support workers need to understand that fulfillment is highly personal and people are much more than their needs. It is challenging since we really don't have an established framework to understand fulfillment.

140

It often takes a long time to understand what a resident wants, but if you make false assumptions all your efforts will lead somewhere they don't want to go. It is important to listen and be objective and get these assumptions right. The issue of fulfillment is important, as you want your residents to be happy. If you start with a misunderstanding of the person your remedy will always be wrong and when you ignore personal needs, you will definitely have consequences. Support workers must ask what is missing in a resident's life. A lot of residents have "small" lives because of their (or other peoples) lack of vision.

141

Engage residents, don't just keep them busy.

142

Staff and resident wellness must be the highest priority. Managers must keep a keen eye for patterns of dysfunction from staff. There is a high rate of addicts in support work. While recovered addicts can make excellent staff, managers need to be aware of the well being of their team. Ideally, managers should even go beyond wellness to consider the deeper issue of fulfillment.

143

Try to find a balance between work, school, recreation, and home in residents' lives. This comes easier with some people than with others. Find out what residents like – what they like to eat, do, listen to, etc., and help them to achieve what they want to do every day. Group homes become lighter and more fun when residents are happy and living balanced lives.

144

The goal is to improve the quality of life of residents and this may be achieved in many different ways. When needs are not properly met, the resident will experience distress, their gifts will be undeveloped, and they will be discontent. Everybody reinvents themselves throughout life and our needs constantly change. Support workers need to understand that everybody has a unique hierarchy of needs and Maslow's "Universal Hierarchy of Needs" is too simplistic. If you are paying attention, most residents will show you what they need.

145

Managing group homes can be tough so be prepared for the highest highs and the lowest lows of your life. Residential care is often an emotional roller coaster for staff and residents, and for managers it can be even worse. It can be the best work and the worst work – sometimes within the same hour. Many find support work to be a short-term vocation, and clearly this type of work appeals to very few people as a life-long career. Staff must be clear about their own wellness and develop strategies to cope with the rigors of the job. If you do good work, your program will usually survive in the long term. Many residents display "pain" behaviors. Being in proximity to people experiencing deep pain can take a toll on caregivers. People in pain are tense and prone to panic. This can lead co-residents and staff to experience vicarious pain if the pain is unattended.

146

Accept the fact that you live in a glass house and will often be criticized by all sides. Commit yourself to providing quality programs and making a difference. Understand that you can be sued or criticized for what you do and what you don't do. Be steady and trust your instincts to provide the best care possible.

147

When you or your program receives criticism, study it and try the criticism on. Is it fair? Does it make sense? Force yourself to be analytical and explore the criticism. And then if an action is required, make the necessary changes and once implemented tell the person that brought the criticism to your attention that changes have been made. The trust that can be achieved by these practices can help transform a program. As a manager that takes criticism well, you will be respected better and gain the confidence of your team. After all, you don't have to be right all the time – just a percentage.

148

Solving other people's problems can be tricky and some of the key programmatic questions you need to always be asking your team are: what does your resident want and what's stopping the resident from reaching this goal? The next question is what is the support team doing to help the resident reach this goal.

149

If your team can be analytical enough to address these questions, your program will likely be on track to get results.

150

The manager needs to know how they will deal with small groups of staff before commencing work. Support workers require leadership that makes sense to them. The accomplishment of quality care is the best reward and is the gas that drives the engine. When a group is focused, they can accomplish great things, and it is the role of the manager to help them act in the best interests of your residents. A team needs to be led with respect and compassion.

151

Support workers can make a meaningful contribution to the lives of their residents. Therefore, handpick a team you respect because this impacts how you lead a team. However, in my experience, positive teams have the bizarre inability to accurately and concisely describe what's working and why it's working. But they work with a sense of accomplishment and pride. And when things are working, you feel as though your team can do anything.

152

When in crisis, a manager can say to the team, "We've hit walls before and we figured it out. And now we've hit another wall, and I know we can figure this out."

You often don't know what the solution will be but you're confident your team will find a solution. And as your team overcomes challenges, they develop an improved ability to deal with bigger challenges.

153

A key management responsibility is motivating staff. This is a very complex task and with some teams seemingly impossible. Generally speaking, working in group homes is low-paid work with limited benefits that results in high staff turnover. There is no alternative than to pay staff adequately and provide realistic benefits and training opportunities. Without these conditions, most group homes falter. After you have established these conditions, many motivational problems tend to evaporate.

Support work can be a highly conceptual and creative job and managers can't motivate with bonuses or other financial incentives to improve productivity. Further, traditional "carrot and stick" rewards and punishment motivators simply don't work in group homes. Complex jobs such as support work require a much more sophisticated motivational approach. In many ways, intrinsic motivators such as mastery and purpose are the best long-term motivators. Seeing a resident improve is an effective reward system in itself, and I can attest to its effectiveness. However, to reach these higher order motivators you must first pay and treat your staff well.

154

Fostering autonomy is an effective way to motivate staff. If your staff work with the premise that working in a group home is chaotic, intellectually unchallenging, and crisis prone, they will likely remain unmotivated. However, if you allow staff to apply their only personalities and problem solving abilities, they will be able to exert their own autonomy and on the whole be more motivated to perform. These conditions lead to more independence by staff and less management is required. An engaging and challenging work environment leads to an improved morale and ultimately more effective workers. These teams find more creative solutions and achieve better results.

155

For many support workers, mastery of their job is the best motivator. These staff are highly skilled and are self motivated because they often get good results. This mastery is often a very individual effort, though it usually depends on feedback from the broader team and management. Mastery and the potential to help are the best motivators in group homes.

156

Managers should concentrate their efforts in helping staff not only make progress but also see progress. Often staff are too close to a problem or involved with a resident to objectively see resident development. Sometimes managers can find empirical measures to show progress but often have to rely on qualitative measures of success.

157

The annual or semi-annual performance evaluation is ridiculous. Imagine an athlete trying to get good at their sport and receiving feedback only once or twice a year – you would never improve. Bureaucracies give annual feedback to cover their asses, but in group homes staff must receive feedback constantly. Staff tend to crave feedback, and it is important for managers to frequently direct and encourage their team. Support workers improve through constant coaching. Motivating staff to perform is a central responsibility of a manager.

158

Managers are time limited and often under resourced. They should try to help the team problem solve and avoid over-managing staff. They must ask themselves where they are making progress and where they are falling behind.

159

Clutter-free homes are easier to clean and more enjoyable to live in. Group homes can easily collect clutter that benefits no one. They need to be organized in meaningful ways with lots of visual reminders and clues. By being clear about expectations, residents can relax easier and accomplish more.

160

Ideally, group homes should be comfortable and aesthetic. Architecture has the ability to foster peace and reduce stress. However, few managers have the luxury of building from scratch with unlimited budgets. Mostly we acquire generic housing that is inexpensive and attempt to make it fit our purposes. While we can make almost anything work, we often don't have the benefit of good interior sight lines, well proportioned rooms, or good views. When acquiring housing, it is best to make a list of desirable attributes and objectively find a building that fits these criteria. What works for a group home is usually very different from what would work for us personally.

161

It is a reality that managers need to be handy. Fortunately, anyone can easily learn basic home handyman skills by taking courses, watching videos, or reading books. As a minimum, managers should be able to repair drywall, paint, and complete trim work. House finish frequently needs repair and touch-ups and these tasks do not require expensive equipment or extensive training to accomplish. By doing the work yourself, you can save a lot of money and get repairs done quicker. However, knowing when to call the professionals is both wise and prudent. Avoid doing any work that could raise safety issues or expensive repairs, such as electrical or plumbing.

162

Most managers started their careers wanting to work with residents but not necessarily managing staff. As a result, few have studied business or management and may be lacking key skills. Managers are responsible for large budgets, the care of often-vulnerable residents, and a host of other things. The politics of being responsible to governments or other boards or committees can only deepen the situation. Managers often inherit poorly developed business plans in a milieu that by its very nature is unpredictable. In the end, this can be a very stressful and brutal way to work.

163

Often it is best to ask your team naïve questions such as "why are we doing this?" or "what does the resident really want?" These sorts of questions allow the team to address the core issues of service delivery and refocus their energies before initiating work.

164

Even if you have a strong team that carefully plans, sometimes your program will go sideways. Managers must first ask the team what is happening and be sure to identify the hurdles or problems. Sometimes you will need to say "we have to stop this now." At these times, you have to be willing to drop the plan and develop an alternate one with the team on short notice. Avoid the urge to make minor changes to salvage the prior effort unless there is a reasonable chance it will succeed another time. Also, it is important to not hold onto old successes too long, as it can lead to a resident's plan collapsing spectacularly. It is a very delicate period and it is usually best to start from scratch and redevelop a new intervention or plan. Your team will usually feel the urgency to replace the old plan in a mad dash, and they need to be led in a paced and orderly discussion. But with humbleness remember that if the team says an idea is terrible, it usually is. If the team doesn't believe in a plan, how well do you think they will follow it?

165

Time and resources in most group homes are scarce and as a result are precious. Managers need to offer the team efficient and actionable support strategies and a cohesive plan of action. The pressure on the manager to accomplish this task can be enormous because the consequences are often weighty. To further complicate matters, it is common for managers to be lobbied by members of the team to support their ideas. Managers must be decisive and strong at these times and understand that mistakes will be made.

166

Staff will often ask what do I do if a resident does something specific. There is rarely only one response. It is important to impress on the staff that the resident must feel respected and safe and that positive supports are the goal rather than hamstringing your team into detailed response plans.

167

State the behavior you expect and tell residents what to do rather than what not to do.

168

There is a difference between being well trained and being gifted. In my career I have worked with a handful of truly gifted support workers. These individuals were breathtaking to watch work. They facilitated activities without the residents knowing they were doing much of anything. However, for the rest of us there is no substitute for good training and orientation. Many people can be trained to be effective support workers given the opportunity for skill development. Managers must provide good training to staff and foster an environment that allows skills to develop. This includes frequent feedback and coaching for skill development.

169

It can be stressful and depressing when your residents are not doing well; therefore, the work environment must strive to be nurturing and supportive of staff. Managers must pick staff up off the floor when things are bad so they are ready for the next challenge. When it is done well, workers have pride and energy.

170

Finally, a group home doesn't suceed if there isn't love involved. We must be passionate about our service and take pride in a job well done. Residents need to know they are connecting with support workers. The ultimate goal is to connect with residents in a meaningful and caring way.

171

Hiring staff is one of the most important decisions a manager will ever face. Since your program is only as good as your front-line staff, recruitment is a weighty and often difficult task. Aside from considerations of relevant experience, education, and the like are other concerns that are equally important. Is the person at the employment interview an independent worker, or will you have to break down their job every day for them? Be clear on what the job is and carefully select the most suitable person you can. Also, give all new hires a probationary period so you have a legitimate way to replace new staff that are not working out.

172

I have worked with many competent, educated, and motivated staff that were incredibly disorganized people. It sometimes feels like you're herding cats, and despite detailed task lists they are incredibly inefficient and ineffective staff. The irony is that organization is a skill that can be learned. To further complicate matters, these individuals are usually very disorganized at home. Due to a lack of planning they tend to have money problems and other difficulties that impact their ability to work effectively. They are the staff that miss shifts due to confusion, accomplish half of the things on To-Do lists that are given to them, forget key tasks, and the like. One of the most important qualities to look for in a potential hire is organizational skill. Therefore, in interviews it is important to gage their organizational abilities. Whether or not they keep To-Do lists at home can be more important to consider than whether they work well in a team environment. Organization is key and many well-intentioned, capable staff will be challenging to work with if they lack this skill. Simply put, avoid hiring disorganized staff.

173

It is sometimes easy for managers to ruminate excessively on their problems. The pressures of the job can be significant and unchanging. These cyclical thoughts are unproductive and can lead to depression and a sense of hopelessness. Keep in mind that living in your repetitive thoughts will not solve the problems you need to solve and will not give you the pleasure of the present moment. You have been hitting yourself in the head with rumination. Put down the hammer and pick up your life.

174

When examining outcome there is a tendency to look for lessons learned. Be really careful when analyzing because there is often at least two lessons to be learned from each experience. And these lessons are often polar opposites depending on your perspective.

175

It is generally believed that people learn from negative consequences; however, this is often a very inefficient way to gain skills and change behaviors.

176

Try not to stress your residents. When stressed, we tend to make poor choices and act erratically. Programs that are based on stressing residents when they make poor choices are ultimately less effective. Group homes should strive to reduce the stress in their resident's lives, not make matters worse.

177

Over time I have learned that I would rather deal with a tyrant than a committee. Sometimes when dealing with a committee it's possible to request the guidance of a single person rather than a group. If you can manage to deal with a single person, you may be able to limit your frustrations immensely.

178

Your goal is not to limit or restrict your team but rather assist them to focus their efforts to be more effective. Replace rules and regulations with principles of service. Eventually you build a pattern of support that allows for greater success.

179

Your job isn't to be perfect; it's to be human. All managers make mistakes and most mistakes don't have dire consequences. Embrace your fallibility and make good, honest mistakes but mostly get things right.

180

There is a cost to not trying and it can be huge and painful.

181

When residents get "stuck" don't concentrate on what they're doing wrong. Instead help them learn productive ways to meet their needs. And remember that any strategy that gives a person choice is always more effective.

182

Talent and ideas are precious. Look for staff who are energetic, enthusiastic, and creative problem solvers. It is critical for managers to find staff that are capable of generating smart and original ideas.

183

Group homes are driven by both staff and resident energy.

184

If you are lucky enough to have a few superb staff, you can accomplish great things. Unfortunately, finding excellent staff is extraordinarily difficult. But in all honesty, I believe there are very few support workers who are given an opportunity to do great work. Become a program that nurtures creativity, professionalism, and excellence, and when you work with great support workers kiss the ground every day in gratitude for having them on your team.

185

I used to think that staff needed years of training to become effective support workers. I now know that staff can contribute at any time in their career. In many ways, the staff with years of experience can be the most dangerous as they may be burned-out or jaded and they may be given too much responsibility. Experience counts but don't overlook rookies with great potential.

186

You want your team to flood residents with positive strategies and reinforcements. By learning to target only truly problem behaviours and using positive support strategies residents learn and grow more easily.

187

It is crucial to help ineffective staff to move on quickly without causing too much damage. Burnout and support fatigue of staff is a big risk in group homes and often one or two limping staff can greatly impact a program's success.

188

If a problematic behaviour is increasing in a group home it almost always being reinforced by staff. Staff should be able to either ignore a behaviour (often referred to as "extinction") or use diversion to channel the problem behaviour.

189

Many staff are damaged and have chosen to work in social services to repair things in their personal lives. This phenomenon is hugely prevalent in the social services field in general, and in many group homes it's endemic. Avoid developing an "enabling" relationship with staff and encourage them to seek outside help if they're struggling.

190

Staff perform best when they feel supported. Management must be aware of this reality and offer staff support on a continuous basis.

191

In many small programs, managers frequently must work with residents on a regular basis. This is an opportunity for managers to display an understanding of what is being requested and role model effective strategies.

192

Staff must learn to not respond negatively to residents behaviour. Neutral responses should replace negative ones at all times. This requires staff to be aware of their body language and the intonation of their voice. Learning to adopt a neutral facade is an important skill for support workers to gain.

193

Support work can be physically dangerous work, especially mental health and youth group homes. Find creative ways to reduce risk wherever possible and seek suggestions from anybody who may offer useful perspectives.

194

Beware of constant stress, as support workers can become both hyper sensitive and desensitized in crisis-prone group homes.

195

It's easy to fall into dysfunctional relationships with residents. It is particularly easy for staff to establish relationships based on staff maintaining power and control.

196

Often group homes don't have a well-developed program model with clearly defined roles and responsibilities. Avoid expecting support workers to "wing it" by developing real program plans with measurable goals.

197

A collaborative approach in group homes works best. Caring for people is a partnership amongst many people, including health professionals, funding agencies, families, residents, and the community. Managers need to carefully consider how they are going to collaborate with their team and with other external supports such as doctors or other professionals and supports.

198

The exchange of day-to-day information needs to be carefully considered. By using technologies like care tracking computer databases, staff can see what other staff are doing, collaborate, brag about successes, etc. – that flattens the hierarchy of a group home. The manager needs to attend to these platforms as opposed to being the one making the decisions. It's more like being the producer of a show rather than being a lead actor. By creating an atmosphere of collaboration, the manager avoids conflict and can dedicate their time more effectively.

199

When you are planning care rule out medical reasons for behaviour by visiting the doctors or other health care professionals.

200

Occasionally I have hired support workers that over time have revealed a lack of insight about their role. This people didn't realize that they lacked expertise and ability. They masked their incompetence by being critical of others and being authoritative and power based with residents. These people had the delusion that they had superior knowledge and therefore had no reason to defer to anyone else's opinion, including management. Their delusion was so complete that it was entirely invisible to them and they increasingly became difficult to work with. Overtime their approaches became more authoritative and disrespectful to residents. If you encounter a staff member with these traits, your program will suffer and I suggest you rid your program of them as quickly as possible.

201

Improve care by involving residents whenever possible. When a resident is consulted they feel they become more invested and things often improve as a result.

202

It's easiest to work in small support teams that blend paid staff with families, advocates, volunteers, etc.

203

When facing budget cuts, your first instinct will always be to try to do more with less. But sometimes the best strategy is just to do less. Stretching an already lean budget to unrealistic extents will not yield satisfactory results.

204

Losing can be good for you.

205

Helping feels great – it's an indescribable high. Let your team experience the feeling of really helping your residents and seeing their lives improve.

206

Your job is really what you make it. You can't wait for somebody to hand you the perfect job. By quickly moving through the less attractive tasks of your job and maximizing the benefit of your program, you can achieve a great deal. Managing a group home is what you make it.

207

Don't try to do too much. If you're an inch deep and a mile wide, you won't get anything done. Concentrate on what you can accomplish and keep objective and optimistic about where to place your energies.

208

A lot of things aren't as complicated as they initially appear. Therefore, it's important to be patient and not rush into solving things.

209

Figuring out how to help someone can be really challenging. For this reason it's important to seek input from every corner of the team.

210

Be a leader and be the heart of your organization. Always be ethical and integral, and do the best job possible. The best leaders role model ethical and consistent work habits.

211

Hold yourself accountable for failure. Learn from your mistakes, apologize, and move forward as a leader.

212

Group homes need to link with schools, businesses, and generic recreation opportunities. The adage "it takes a community" is apt, and managers should make an effort to access as many community opportunities as possible. The goal should be to develop a cluster of services and pursuits outside of paid social services staff and specialized programming. Many residents have staff contact but don't have networks in the community to support them. Personally, I've been astonished by how many group homes underuse generic community resources. In this instance, we can increase support by accessing community-based services and opportunities. Many great ideas come from the broader team as they're not so wedded to day-to-day issues of the resident. Residents need a support network beyond paid caregivers, and by accessing generic opportunities in the community they can more readily achieve this.

212

Many behaviors are predictable. With experience, managers usually gain the ability to sense them coming. The best predictor of future behavior is past behavior, and in time you will see many behaviors as repetitious and predictable. The relevant question then becomes if you know what will trigger a given behavior, should you remove the trigger? Or do you simply work on the expression of the behavior and try to guide it into adaptive expressions?

213

Help residents "unlearn" problem behaviors by substituting more adaptive behaviors. Many inappropriate behaviors have been learned and are entrenched. Trying a new behavior can be scary and a struggle for many residents as they often don't consider their behaviors as a choice. All behavior is purposeful and once we understand the root cause of the behavior, support workers can help the resident with developing better expressions of that behavior. Often, this is a very slow process that requires careful planning and continuous support. This is a skill that your team must grow adept with encouraging.

214

Be immediate, fresh, and fun as much as possible. These characteristics are attractive to staff and residents alike. When residents feel happy and challenged, they achieve greater things. For this reason, staff must avoid being adversarial or skeptical with residents. Many staff I have encountered need to lighten up and have more fun with colleagues and residents. Overall, life in a group home should be fun for support workers and residents, and when it is not fun this should be evaluated and adjustments made immediately.

215

Encourage and establish a unique relationship with each resident and ensure that the resident knows that they really matter.

216

Even when excelling, help clients and staff take it to the next level. Managers need to concentrate on success as much as they do on failure. When you immerse yourself in good programming you sometimes see things differently, and this can lead to even greater success.

217

Develop a reputation of responsible risk taking in order to help the resident and staff succeed. By planning to take risks and make mistakes, we unhitch from achieving "success" all the time. Caregivers must expect setbacks and concentrate on bouncing back when things don't work out as hoped or planned. Many of the situations in group homes are an experiment as everybody has different backgrounds and aptitudes, and what works for one person doesn't work for another. By embracing risk taking as a core reality, the manager will help the team achieve greater success.

218

Support workers should have access to contractual standards of care and related administrative material. This will help the team understand expectations.

219

Residents communicate in thousands of different ways and staff must be open minded in teasing out what they are saying. Much communication is non-verbal and even behaviour is a type of communication.

220

Making progress with residents is the best motivator for support workers. Managers should concentrate their efforts in helping staff not only make progress, but also see progress of residents.

221

Group home managers often struggle with where to put their energy and limited resources. The relevant question is what are the goals of the program? Where is the manager and the team making progress and where are they falling behind? Managers must develop the ability to appraise their program and encourage the team to develop self-assessment skills, as well. This is a challenging prospect because the manager and the team often lacks objectivity. By developing these skills, the team will become more independent and effective and this will hopefully translate into enhanced results.

222

Trying to follow your instincts sounds easy, but often isn't.

223

Sometimes you have staff that have proven themselves effective in the past but are now pulling up short and not performing. In these cases it's always best to make the staff feel supported while you let them know what you are observing. Much of the time it's possible to help them remedy their short comings by intervening and these efforts will be most effective if applied as soon as possible.

224

Sometimes a team proposes an idea that they will likely be unable to follow through on in the long term. A manager needs to ask them whether the strategy is sustainable and help them find alternatives.

225

Dogs have an important role in group homes. Dogs that are friendly, affectionate, and non-aggressive can warm-up the most disenfranchised resident. I've seen the demeanor of residents improve as soon as a dog walks through the door. Encourage staff to bring their own pets to work or volunteer to walk dogs from the animal shelter. Keep a water dish and big bag of treats and kibble to encourage staff to bring their dogs to work. Consider building a dog run in a back yard with closeline and long leash so the dog can spend time outside and alone when needed.

226

If the team says an idea is terrible, it usually is.

227

Don't be afraid to ask your team naïve questions. These sorts of questions can help keep the team's feet on the ground.

228

When support workers are doing well, you know it. You see a spark in the way they interact with residents and the things they accomplish.

229

Sometimes the wheels fall off the bus. Failure is unavoidable and part of the process.

230

Be prepared to drop the plan when it's not working and be willing and able to develop a new one on short notice.

231

Don't be lured to make minor changes to salvage a plan that's not working. This often happens when you hold onto old successes too long as it can lead to a person's care collapsing very broadly and sometimes spectacularly. Sometimes you need to say "we have to stop this now"and then make bold changes to move forward.

232

There is no one way. As humbling as this is, keep this phrase on your mind at all times. A manager's job isn't for support workers to complete tasks their way all the time but rather to achieve clearly defined goals. Support workers will do things their way and that is natural and understandable.

233

Staff will often ask what to do if a resident does this or that. There is rarely only one response, and it is important to impress on the staff that the resident must feel respected and safe and that positive interactions are to be used. Some staff get paralyzed by uncertainty and need encouragement to proceed. The goal of the manager at these times should be to support the staff to work effectively with independence and freedom. Afterwards, check in with the staff and make sure they are feeling okay.

234

Residents need clear and reasonable goals and support workers must clearly state the behavior they expect. It's always best to tell residents what to do rather than what not to do, and try to be as positive as possible. Many defiant residents only require gentle encouragement in this respect. By reinforcing the fact that they are being monitored, they can very quickly achieve goals.

235

Sometimes you look at a resident's program plan and you have to ask whether anyone in the room really believes it is a good solution with a realistic chance of success.

236

As caregivers, we must always remember that residents can get healthier, learn new skills, develop more positive behaviors, and grow in all ways.

237

Generally speaking, residents like group homes more if they understand what is being expected of them and they are having fun. Bad group homes are dangerous places where creativity is suppressed and souls are deadened. But when it's done well, a good group home is a celebration of the human spirit. When it is done well, workers have pride and energy.

238

In many ways it all comes down to your front-line staff. That is where the rubber hits the road. It doesn't matter how enlightened or well intentioned a manager is if they have a discouraged and disconnected staff. Over the years I've met staff from all over the spectrum. I've met burned-out, negative staff who blame residents for everything and see them as the "problem." On the other hand, there are also those generous-hearted folks who genuinely want the people who they care for to succeed and grow. Obviously it is critical to weed out the jaded and damaged staff as quickly and as unapologetically as possible. Managers need to build teams of healthy and motivated staff that take direction and bring heart and soul to their work.

239

A lot of the people I have worked with have had traumatic childhoods. Being raised in a home with violence, addiction or other circumstances, makes support work much more challenging. One of the most important things a team must do upon intake is understand that these early lives have left an indelible, lifelong impact on these individuals. While there is still love in these homes, they are often not supportive places where individuals can grow and reach their potential.

240

As caregivers we must identify residents that are traumatized and offer them services that are caring and effective. The traumatized resident often has a generalized inability to cope with average stressors. Their response is often panicky and primal and can easily withdraw into depression or become violent. To be effective, caregivers must deal with trauma in proactive ways and seek out professional support as required. At the very least, we should avoid retraumatizing residents and strive to assist and improve their situation.

241

Programs with the least amount of training and staff support tend to be the ones that use the most physical restraints and other intrusive interventions. Capable and motivated teams tend to prevent these escalated situations and the frequency and intensity of the crisis are lessened.

242

Often by the time a resident reaches care they have lived under horrible circumstances for a very long time. Once in care, they are shuffled between multiple living environments before landing somewhere they can live for a period of time. The subsequent issues of attachment and loss can fuel secondary states of depression and defiance.

243

To get a resident to attach to care can be a tricky and continuous effort. Caregivers must allow residents to direct their care as much as possible and offer them support at every effort. However, the trick is to offer them support for their emotional or functional needs and try not to rob them of independence or enable them in any way. And this is the trick: the best workers will be able to establish a trust relationship that may be adversarial at times but ultimately has deep bonds. This is a very tricky thing and managers must extend a lot of room for the workers to do their thing. Managers must closely monitor their workers and debrief them whenever required.

244

Currently there isn't a lot of agreement in a treatment model for dealing with trauma residentially. Undoubtedly much research needs to be done but in the meantime we can point to a few approaches that may offer at least some relief. For years I have seen support workers offer care to traumatized residents without formally identifying their approaches as being trauma-based and they've been somewhat effective.

245

The goal of all programs should be the long-term outcome of its residents. Every other goal pales in importance and the team must rally around the effort to ensure the best possible outcome for its residents.

246

Generally speaking, most programs spend most of their effort on social skill and interpersonal development of residents. To be able to address these concerns, we must work with residents on their trauma and help them relax and adjust to the artificial environments we have built for them. This is no easy task for the majority of residents and it's best to think of these goals as often being lifelong struggles for the many residents.

247

By prioritizing goals, we can help our teams focus and assist residents in a more organized and effective practice. Many residents will struggle with the basics of independent living. Without a foundation that is grounded in attachment, they can master individual skills but often have difficultly connecting all these elements into a cohesive, effective whole. Often it is the soft skills of confidence, creativity, and perseverance that are the most obvious culprits. The question then crops up as to how best to teach these skills.

248

Clearly play has a huge role in group homes. The beauty of play is that it can allow residents and staff to relax and explore complex interpersonal relationships. It also allows them to exhaust their nervous energy and settle down. For this reason, most programs should encourage significant physical activity and play every day. The benefits of play are well established and studied and should never be ignored.

249

Another benefit of play is that many inexperienced staff can engage residents meaningfully with limited training or monitoring from management. It allows for deep relationships between staff and residents to develop and injects a healthy amount of fun into any program. Children learn many skills through play and role modeling and this is true of residents as well. It also allows residents to develop relationships amongst themselves that are based on friendship and mutual enjoyment.

250

In my experience, there is a huge variability of outcomes for residents that are not entirely based on cognitive functioning. I have seen many residents with high functioning levels live very limited lives because of missing social skills, low self esteem, a lack of confidence. By not trying new things or exploring their potential, they sometimes remain pessimistic and unhappy. The question remains as to how we reach these individuals to help them live fuller, more independent lives.

251

While cognitive levels cannot realistically be improved, it is possible to help residents to improve their attitude to live more rich lives. Non-cognitive skills such as perseverance or commitment can be enhanced through play, repetition, and encouragement. When residents enter care, it is common for them to display behaviors like defiance or even depression. By concentrating on non-cognitive skills, huge inroads towards greater independence and fulfillment can be achieved.

252

The use of medications needs to be carefully considered, as they offer significant benefits and sometimes significant risks. Medications are a reality for many in care, and it is common for people to enter care with a complicated daily medication regime. With some individuals, their anxiety or depression or other conditions are too significant and dampen efforts to reach them. Through the careful use of medication, it is possible to assist them break down their walls and learn new skills. I have seen many youth diagnosed as hyperactive and prescribed Ritalin and other medications. Deep down I know these children could benefit from rigorous physical activity and a plan of care that includes reducing their anxiety and trauma-related behaviors. The over use of medications for relatively common conditions such as depression and ADHD shouldn't limit our ability to see medications for what they are: another tool that can yield significant benefits.

253

Medication side effects need to be well understood by the team. Therefore, it's important to take careful notes so the doctor can tailor dosage. Pharmacists can provide much important information and their input should always be sought when new medications are prescribed or the dosage of the medication changed.

254

Many group homes seem to struggle with the notion of teaching conduct. That is, those behaviors that are socially normative. In this area, my opinions are somewhat conservative. I feel many people in care need to be encouraged to act "politely" and "properly." Some residents come from backgrounds where conduct wasn't emphasized, while others may use their conduct to express their defiance. I feel it is important to teach and expect residents to be polite and considerate in their conduct. This social skill is highly misunderstood and leads many to feelings of low self-esteem because they don't understand how others perceive their manners or behavior. Staff need to be clear about social expectations and work towards a high level of conduct from residents at all times. Swearing should be discouraged.

It is possible to work on these soft skills concurrently with hard skills like school or employment; however, this will always be a balancing game. It is incredibly easy to overwhelm residents if we over program them with school, work, or home. The priority should always be interpersonal development, as this will lead to far greater success in the long run. An individual who is prone to anger will always be limited in what they can achieve in the short-term because frustration is often a by-product of learning. Through effective treatment and repetition of skill development, these soft skills can be learned and eventually they will settle into a pattern of success.

255

Because many residents have been treated as "different"or as "problems" by the education or justice system, their birth families, or their placement families, they often have low self esteem and lack confidence. A significant emphasis in any program is needed to bolster their fragile confidence and to broaden their horizons as to what is possible. This process has to extend well beyond praising them at every turn and instead allowing them to explore new experiences in a supportive environment.

256

Residents have to be taught perseverance and not to quit too easily. I have worked with many residents who are quick to say "I quit" or "I can't." Teaching perseverance and resilience are very complicated endeavors, and there are many different approaches and techniques support workers can use. In any plan of care, this issue needs to be carefully considered and outcomes measured. Like Sisyphus moving the rock up the hill, anything is possible, and residents need to be encouraged to persevere with all tasks.

257

Many residents struggle with delayed gratification. Residents with disabilities such Fetal Alcohol Effect are notorious for their inability to delay gratification. Any condition with memory deficits is going to be challenged with delayed gratification. Support workers must identify these character traits and explore the individual's ability to learn this skill. Some residents with even the most elaborate programs seem to always act impulsively and teams must acknowledge what is changeable and what is not. Sometimes identifying a deficit like this and adjusting an individual's environment is the most effective approach. For this reason, when working with diabetics with poor impulse control, we lock kitchen cabinets.

258

For individuals coming from troubled homes, it is important to seek support for their parents or siblings as well. If your family is troubled, it may be impossible for an individual to be entirely successful and they are likely to feel depressed and/or anxious. Considering that the support worker is a point of contact for social services for a family, it is possible to establish a trust relationship and then connect the family with needed services or support. This also goes for pets, for instance. Many food banks offer pet food, and it may be calming for the person in care to know their cherished dog is being cared for. This is an important consideration and can lead to much trust being established.

259

Most residents benefit from an organized lifestyle. Bed times, meal times, and wake times need to be established with an expectation that resident will follow simple routines. Many residents enter care from very chaotic home backgrounds. Once established, residents will be better able to function, as they will be more clear headed and rested. The defiant ones will rebel but over time and with supportive correction they will feel more settled and better able to succeed at work, school, and life in general. While it is important to respect choice it is my opinion that most residents function better with a sympathetic structure imposed on them. Many residents will rebel either initially or continually, and this will create an adversarial relationship with staff. But this is a battle you want to have. Most residents reluctantly crave structure and its benefits will be clear and obvious to the resident over time. There are good battles and bad battles to have with residents, and this is a good one to have. For instance, parents often battle with children to get them to go to bed on time. The parents know that a tired child will not be able to function the next day if they don't go to bed on time. Therefore, an effective parent will enforce a bedtime routine out of the desire to have a happier, more capable child. Support workers should see this pursuit similarly.

260

Stress is a huge issue and needs to be considered throughout every day. Residents should be encouraged to engage in physical activity from the time they wake up until the time they go to sleep. An effort should be made to de-stress the house by keeping it uncluttered and as quiet as possible. In the evening, lights should be dimmed to encourage relaxation before sleep.

261

You have to figure out how to engage residents, and when something is working lean into whatever it is and make it work. A frequent question to your team must always be the preferences and likes of all your residents. Once you know what they like and what their desires are, they will be easier to engage. Offering programs based on their interests are more successful and yield many benefits.

262

If you don't have any applicants with an obviously suitable education or background, take a second look at their resumes. I have had great luck employing people with a diversity of backgrounds. For instance, a person with experience as a swimming instructor is used to working with people who are frightened and they know how to break down skill training into many small steps.

263

Train yourself to motivate good work from your team.

Praise often and offer support unconditionally and freely. Personally, I love visiting my team and helping with mundane chores. I frequently mow lawns or wash vans as an appreciation of the team's commitment and to show them that I want to participate at all levels.

264

The people who work hardest in an honest and open way usually succeed. In many cases, hard work is the best indicator of success. Also, having the team seeing you work hard is a motivator. By role modeling commitment and effort, you set a tone for your team and there isn't any substitute for it. Having your manager sleeping in her office, going home early, and earning more money can rot the soul out of a team. Work hard and let everybody know that you expect a good effort from them as well.

265

Success breeds success. Some have called this "the winner effect" and it describes how sometimes a team or an individual will have a prolonged string of successes. When it's happening, it is a great feeling and much progress can be made. It's important for managers to assist the advancements made during periods of success.

266

It's far easier for small teams to gain skills and create success with residents. Trying to train and lead a large team often feels unwieldy and overwhelming, and for this reason try to keep teams as small as possible. The results may surprise you.

267

Encourage your team to spend the first half hour of their workday reading other staff member's notes from previous shifts and planning their day accordingly. Encourage them to research anything that pertains to their job. Planning and collaborating at the start of their shift will encourage greater success and achievement because they may be able to implement different strategies and approaches.

268

It's not advantageous to subscribe to print journals any more. The team should be encouraged to research online and create a collection of material that may benefit the broader team. The benefit of online research is that there aren't any subscription fees and a wide range of material is available. Staff should use their "downtime" both in the group home and on mobile devices when they are waiting at swimming pools or other venues with residents.

269

Find tools to allow your team to do their work efficiently and thoroughly. Productivity really matters in group homes.

270

Take management training whenever you can. There is always something to learn and a short workshop can jump start your performance when you are stuck.

271

Running a group home can be challenging, so make sure to take care of yourself. That includes eating right, getting exercise, and sleeping. You can't help others nearly as effectively if you don't take care of yourself. Therefore, make sure to consider your own personal wellbeing on a constant basis.

272

Use data to support your decisions and ultimately your program to families and outside agencies. If your team is collecting the right information, this shouldn't be difficult.

273

Think long-term with staff and residents. By committing to them you will be more willing to invest time and energy.

274

Email is not a secure place to discuss confidential information. By it's very nature, email can be easily hacked and the results can be disastrous. Instead, design in-house IT systems behind firewalls that function similarly to email but protect the conversation. Some databases provide this ability and there are stand alone products, as well.

275

When dealing with funding agencies, make sure to

promote your business's value and performance and not just its costs.

276

Let information flow throughout the team.

277

Both growth and downsizing need to be carefully considered. There are many false economies in group homes and finding the best size for your organization takes much planning and study. Many group home businesses tend to be micro businesses or large concerns. This polarizing makes sense because when a group home is relatively small the manager can more easily control operations. Larger businesses benefit from a much more diverse infrastructure with a lot of role specialization. Both small, independent group homes and much larger businesses have their relative benefits. That said, it's important to consider your motivations for changing the scale of your organization. Often crisis is the motivation to grow or downsize, and this is sometimes a poor choice. Don't grow for growth's sake – many teams and group homes scale poorly.

278

Stand up for your suppliers by giving business to neighborhood businesses if you can. You are trying to build a community and local businesses are part of that community. Group homes spend a lot of money on groceries and supplies, and it's best to build local relationships with other small businesses.

279

The problem with uncertainty is it can lead to fear.

280

Study how other group homes face similar problems to yours. Often you can borrow insights and approaches that have a better chance of success.

281

Partner with advocates to promote the goals of your group home.

282

It is really easy for some staff to convince themselves they see things they don't. They want to believe their client's growth is real and can really believe what they think they are seeing and overlook the facts.

283

In group homes speed really counts. Consult with your team, make decisions quickly, and implement them as soon as possible. Change hurts but indecision kills, and over time most managers learn to make decisions on the fly. By adjusting quickly, you empower your team to consult and make course corrections frequently.

284

Build on your program's strengths.

285

Be honest and open to your team at all times. Speaking from the heart can drive home any message. If your team feels you are always honest, they will more readily accept your suggestions and support. They don't necessarily need to agree with you all the time, but if they feel you are consulting and basing your decisions on data they are more likely to be supportive.

286

Good support workers don't always make good managers, though promoting from within your team is wonderful when it works out. You end up with a manager that really understands the nitty gritty of the group home and can empathize with support workers. However, not all support workers make good managers. Being a manager is very different from being a support worker. Sometimes job training and orientation can resolve these issues. Other times it is a problem of workplace suitability and no amount of effort can resolve this reality.

287

How people handle one situation is a good indicator of how they'll handle other situations. When I hire new staff I often task them with something that I closely monitor. How they handle this one task is a surprisingly accurate way of gauging how they will handle other situations. If they are focused and efficient, you may have struck gold. However, if they leave the task undone you may have a situation on your hands.

288

The bulk of the crisis in group homes tends to happen in the evenings and on weekends. During the week, residents tend to go to school or work, and after hours when the house is full, things really start to kick. Therefore, being accessible to your team means being available when crisis happens and that means weekends and evenings. If you can't be there personally, be available on the phone or video conferencing (e.g., Skype or FaceTime). The purpose of these interventions is rarely to set policy but rather to develop a response to a crisis situation.

289

Whenever a team member raises a question or concern, address it as quickly as possible. But don't stop there. If required, do online searches or other consults and share these perspectives with the team member. Allow them to see that you take their opinion seriously and try to allow the conversation to continue when possible.

290

The residential care field is undergoing significant change and seeking ways to adapt. As a model of care, group homes have only been around for fifty years. In this time they have undergone significant changes and will continue to evolve. Therefore, it's important to keep your organization flexible and adaptable to these changes. As Darwin said, it's not the biggest or strongest that survives but the most adaptable. Managers need to keep their knowledge of the industry current and be willing to adapt to changing conditions. Strive to keep your team flexible to the changing needs of residents and the community.

291

Look at your organization through other people's eyes. Consider what your organization looks like to its residents or families that it serves. How do you think neighbors see your group home? How do social workers see your program? By trying to visualize how others may see your program, you can gain valuable insights and make adjustments accordingly.

292

Optimize your team's learning by providing useful information, news, and resources. Offer to pay for training and participation forums as you're able. An informed team is more likely to engage in their work. The more masterfully the team is able to do their job, the more engaged they will be about their work. Even the most skillful and qualified team member can benefit from training.

293

Try not to be an introvert by spending too much time in your office. Most of the meaningful work in group homes happens on the floor, so make sure you spend a lot of time in communal spaces providing feedback and support.

294

If you generate To-Do lists in team meetings, follow up with posting these lists on staff bulletin boards or online using the various To-Do list hosting services. The benefit of posting online is it allows for quick updates and subsequent discussion. To-Do lists are important as they show an effort is being made to improve programming.

295

Some information is meant to be private and it's important that it is stored in a way to preserve privacy. Examples of this type of information include payroll information, company financial statements, written reprimands, and employment applications. Not only should computer systems be password protected, but also file cabinets should be locked and sensitive documents always kept secure. Privacy can be easily achieved through organized office systems and rigid adherence to privacy protocols. For this reason, all staff should be briefed on privacy and sign confidentiality covenants.

296

Try to be likeable. I'm not saying you don't have to be yourself but being liked will always help you gain traction with your team. While not everybody will like you, it is important to try to put your best face forward. You don't want to be the manager that your team despises.

297

Avoid hiring "yes men." Having opposition within the team is healthy and beneficial for managers. You want a team that will challenge you and not blindly follow your direction to the detriment of your program.

298

You must always be open for the unplanned. When unexpected opportunities present themselves, you must take advantage of them.

299

Let ideas and plans combine in unexpected and surprising ways. Life isn't simple and you must allow your plans to morph and grow. It's impossible to anticipate all the twists and turns.

300

Everybody knows something you don't. Accept that absolutely everybody has a perspective that can offer you insight and an improved understanding.

301

There is a link between morale and productivity so try to keep your team happy. If your team is unhappy, take a few of them out for a coffee and ask them what's the matter. Don't dominate the conversation; this is their opportunity to guide you to improve things. You may be surprised by the insights you're given so plan to take plenty of notes.

302

Post mortem bad decisions and crisis but don't place blame.

303

It's a universal truth that in group homes you will achieve eighty percent of your results from twenty percent of your effort. I'm unsure why this is the case, but in my experience it's the reality. The unfortunate truth is you rarely know what strategies are going to work so you have to try lots of different things.

304

Set clear and reasonable goals with residents. State the behavior you expect and tell residents what to do rather than what not to do

305

There is a difference between staff that are well trained and the ones that are truly gifted. Both are good but the gifted staff are great. They accomplish incredible things every shift and are effortless to manage. The problem is they are truly rare people. You can still accomplish great things with well-trained staff but you will notice when you are in the presence of greatness. When you are, savor it and appreciate your good fortune.

306

When it's done well, a good group home is a celebration of the human spirit. When it's done well, workers have pride and energy. You don't want any part of a failing group home. As soon as you walk through the door, they feel "off" and are miserable places to live in and work in. Avoid these places at all costs.

307

Some people seem impervious from learning from their experiences and the consequences of their actions.

You need to love being a group home manager to be truly effective. We must be passionate about our service and take pride in a job well done. When things go poorly, you will need this passion to push through obstacles. Long, stressful hours of work will likely be required and only people with real fire will be able to persevere.

308

Learn to take criticism with grace. When governments give dumb suggestions or unfair criticism, take notes. Not only does it help you hide your pain or aggravation, but it also gives the message that you are listening. State your point of view but don't get locked into a power struggle you can't come close to winning. Remember that when dealing with governments, you will often be the only person in the room that can lose their job. In meetings, state your position, take notes, and try not to make enemies.

309

Learn to identify the weak government administrators, and when possible avoid them like the plague. They're the ones that give vague solutions to complicated problems. Assume they haven't read their files or are unable to remember them. They often act aggressively to hide their ineptness and insecurity because at some level they know they're incompetent. Meetings with them are worse than pointless because they will expect you to act on their idiotic ideas and half thoughts. The sad truth is these people rarely move and you may have to deal with them for the rest of your career. For this reason, consider your potentially long-term relationship and like any bad marriage let things go unsaid because they're never going to change or listen anyways.

310

There's a big difference between evil administrators and genuinely incompetent administrators. Both are trouble but evil administrators are much, much worse. Evil administrators get a high bringing pain and suffering to people that work with them. If you get in a fight with an evil administrator, you will almost always lose so always avoid conflict with these people. And if by chance you win the fight, they will pound you into the ground in many other ways you can't even imagine.

311

There is no such thing as being a harmless, idiotic group home manager. Don't ever be this person. If you can't be a good manager, do something else. Quit your job and wait tables, drive a cab, or sell furniture. Do anything else.

312

Discourage your residents from playing violent or sexually overt video games. I'm unsure what the research says, but who cares, it's ugly and really doesn't belong in group homes.

313

Develop an ability to accurately critique the work of your staff. By seeing strengths and weaknesses, you can help them develop and hone skills. Mastery of a job is a great motivator as nothing drains a person's energy more than doing a poor job.

314

When given suggestions by government administrators, make a commitment to incorporate as many of the better ideas as possible. You will make enemies very quickly by appearing to dismiss suggestions – even the moronic ones. That said, never do anything that will damage or weaken your program. These situations require an open mind and a delicate touch.

315

Many meetings with government administrators don't accomplish much and don't make the mistake of taking them too seriously. If your program is strong, you usually have enough momentum to make the worst meetings feel like mere speed bumps.

316

Always be polite and respectful to everybody. Make it your policy and encourage every member of your team to act similarly. It is more than good manners as it makes your program more accessible to outsiders.

317

Nobody likes a cry baby. In meetings state your opinion clearly and succinctly, and don't expect any follow-up on many of your concerns. You'll just be setting yourself up to be disappointed if you become too impassioned.

318

Government has a short memory for all the times you take a resident that is "difficult to place" and then struggle with his inappropriate placement for eighteen months. Stepping outside your comfort zone to address their lack of planning often leads to disappointing results for everybody, especially the resident.

319

Be the type of person your team can count on at all times. Be available and pitch in whenever you're needed.

320

Every staff has potential to grow and learn. The problem is they sometimes don't know what they need and neither do you. If staff are motivated and have potential, pull out all the stops in assisting them to improve their performance.

321

Being a manager teaches you there are lots of things you cannot control. For instance, many decisions are dictated by government policy when you're not even in the room. The one thing you can do is work creatively and as hard as possible and effect change where you can.

322

Lean on your database to support decision making. For this reason, your team needs to be encouraged to track the right things and to watch overall trends. Interpreting data can be tricky; however, you have to be extremely careful not to rely on wrong or misleading information. Some outcomes are subtle and can take years to show up in your data.

323

Sometimes trying to reason with people doesn't work. It's not that you're not communicating well or have a good case, it's just that not all problems can be resolved this way.

324

Learn to let go of ideas and strategies that are ineffective.

325

Managers quickly learn that people choose what they want to hear. When doing performance reviews of your team, this becomes readily apparent.

326

When you start out, most managers' performance is weak and many rookie mistakes are made. It takes time to find your way so be patient with yourself and try to learn from your mistakes. You'll be making lots of them.

327

Everybody deserves a second chance.

328

Understand that for most residents being in care sucks. They want to be home with their family or living independently.

329

Post a map of your neighborhood in a communal place so staff and residents can easily orient themselves.

330

Place wall clocks and calendars in places where everybody can easily see them.

331

Keep an emergency stash of clothing and toiletries. If staff deal with an ill resident or have another type of crisis, they may need a shower and a change of clothing. Going to Walmart for a stash of sweats and toiletries is a small price to thank staff for going above and beyond.

332

One of the most dangerous aspects of support work is driving residents. For this reason, orient staff to every vehicle and make sure the vehicles are in good working order at all times. If you are driving any residents that may distract the driver, take a second staff member to assist. Driving residents anywhere at anytime should be approached with caution.

333

Devices such as garburators are accidents waiting to happen and should be removed from group homes. For this reason, group homes should be as safe and uncluttered as possible. I'm a big believer in having LCD TV's affixed to walls and over-balance protectors added to bookcases, and so on.

334

If you or your team use their own personal vehicle for work, make sure it is safe and insured to cover this use. Also, make sure the company pays a reasonable mileage fee.

335

Have a technician annually check all household appliances for wear and tear. Group homes almost always have commercial kitchens and things wear out quickly. Check the fridge and freezer temperatures and look for worn-out gaskets, seals, and belts. Clothes driers cause many house fires and the vents need to be cleaned regularly to keep them safe.

336

Try to think like a sports coach. Keep an eye on things and help staff perform their best by offering continuous advice and encouragement. When a mistake is made, help them shake it off quickly and get back to work.

337

Avoid posting "house rules," as they make the house look custodial and are usually ignored by the people they are meant to encourage. For instance, everybody knows they can't smoke inside and signs aren't necessary. If you have house rules, give residents copies and let them keep them in the privacy of their bedrooms.

338

When staff aren't on breaks, they should be encouraged to be always working. There is always work to be done in a group home. Staff will develop and maintain skills through committed effort. However, encourage your team to work at a steady pace and take regular breaks.

339

Great support workers understand that they are often the most impactful while doing other things. Sometimes the best discussions with residents happen on the drive back from the swimming pool or when waiting for the laundry to be done. Many residents are kinesthetic and open up when they are on walks or distracted with other tasks.

340

There are lots of "experts" that will offer suggestions on running your group home. I've found that the best suggestions come from experienced group home managers with a record of running good programs. If possible, invite these people to lunch or for a coffee and pick their brains. They have much to offer you as they are the real experts. Remember to bring a pad of paper and always pick up the check.

341

Conferences have as much harmful advice as useful advice and should be approached with an open but critical mind.

342

The easiest place to start with motivating staff is to consider wages and benefits. Simply put, it is important to take care of your staff materially so you can work on other issues. Most group homes spend more than three quarters of their income on wages and benefits. It is important for managers to operate lean programs so they can pay their staff as well as possible. Many group homes struggle with poor staffing and high turnover because they pay poorly. It is impossible to have an effective team unless managers can take care of their teams. Support workers must be ensured of a decent income and medical care. Guarantee your team that they will be treated with respect and dignity. It is only once you take these things off the table that you can establish the higher-order things.

343

Never forget that every staff member and every resident is unique. Each person has their own individual way of doing things, and it's important to accept this reality as a strength. Staff must always respond to residents truthfully and honestly.

344

Encourage your team to be adaptable, immediate, and fun.

345

Learn from your team and your residents – they are your very best teachers. Try to learn while you're working and never give up.

346

Many of the best support workers have the ability to notice patterns of behavior and make connections between complex observations. If a manager can develop this skill, they will be hugely successful.

347

Don't hesitate to try to trace behaviors back to their origins. This can yield surprising results if you avoid being judgmental or simplistic in your thinking.

348

When you or your team makes mistakes, don't hide them. Make sure everyone knows them and you learn from them and don't repeat the mistake. For this reason, it's important to develop an open and honest dialogue with your staff and residents.

349

Group homes are interconnected and complicated places to work and live.

350

The primary goal in the evolution of group homes must be to erode the binary of support worker/resident. Teams must always include residents in their focus. Staff should never be the sole decision makers separate from residents. By broadening out decision making, we instinctively increase potential and outcome.

351

Teams need to be encouraged to share as much as possible. Seasoned staff need to have an opportunity to orient and train newer staff on a continual basis. Likewise, staff with fresh ideas need to share new approaches and tech-niques. A team that shares freely is a healthier team.

352

The strongest teams are always collaborative and respon-sive. Find ways to enhance communication between sup-port workers. The weekly or bi-weekly team meeting is often a strangely ineffective way to collaborative. A few individuals often dominate team meetings and many opin-ions and ideas don't get raised. Posting agendas that any-body can add to helps. However, I am skeptical of the value of team meetings and feel there are better ways to encourage collaboration. For instance, we use a social media tool on our database.

353

Group homes need discussion and engaged and thoughtful staff. Boilerplate responses need to be replaced with dis-cussion. Managers should strive to deepen relationships with residents and staff and promote positive discussions.

354

There are many studies that show seclusion and restraint can cause lifelong emotional damage to residents. It can also traumatize support workers and lead to crippled rela-tionships with residents. Programs that practice seclusion and restraint tend to be broken group homes. Staff with the least training, lowest pay, and least support tend to be much more likely to use seclusion and restraint. For these reasons, these practices need to be avoided. If we believe all behavior is purposeful, we must also see behaviors as adaptations. Teams that problem solve creatively where they avoid the use of restraints have the most success at preventing crisis.

355

Most day programs strive for paid employment as part of a normalized goal. They often also believe in micro enterprise, volunteerism, and cultural contribution.

356

Social media like Facebook has a lot of benefit to residents. It encourages them to have a productive day so they have something to write about. It is age appropriate and can allow for meaningful social interaction and discourse. However, many residents need support using social media and being appropriate.

357

People living in group homes have the same capacity to enjoy life and be fulfilled as anyone else. Life is fulfilling when we explore our passions and interests and these pursuits are highly motivating and sustaining. For that reason, we must be continually observing and asking residents about their interests in an effort to understand what makes them feel fulfilled. There is a tendency to look at residents as being the sum of their needs. But people are much more than their needs.

358

Don't hide your faults – most people working with you will see them anyways. If you tend to be disorganized, strive to be more organized but don't pretend you're not the disorganized mess that you are. By showing that you have weaknesses that you struggle with, you display humility and insight. You know there is a problem in your performance and you are trying to improve. That is what we ask of staff, isn't it?

359

Don't be afraid to get your hands dirty. I have found some of the best work has been achieved when a toilet overflows. It's not pleasant, but somebody has to work the plunger and showing the team that you will pitch in is deeply meaningful.

360

Encourage your team to be leaders. By being a strong team leader, you are role modeling and this is an important way people learn. Promoting team members from within has many advantages, and key staff that are performing well should be encouraged to take greater responsibilities within the organization. These individuals should be encouraged to attend courses, workshops, or conferences to enhance these skills. By paying for these courses, you are further saying that you believe in their potential.

361

Strive to be an empathetic leader that is knowledgeable and experienced. You want to surprise your team by always being accessible and willing to pitch in. Your team needs to know that you will do whatever is needed and that you will fight for them. Achieving this balance and subtle understanding can be a challenge, but there is no substitution for it.

362

Learn to ask your staff this simple question: "How can I help?" Often there isn't anything you can do, but by asking this question you are saying that you want to help and you respect and understand their efforts.

363

When managers get worn out and disillusioned, they often stop taking care of themselves and their work suffers immeasurably. For this reason, the best managers are very self aware and strive to always maintain their personal wellness. If a manager crashes, their program starts to feel the effects right away. Do yourself a favor and make sure you eat well, get exercise, and seek whatever supports are required to stay healthy. Seek the advice of a trusted psychologist or colleague if you are feeling overwhelmed or worn out. By being self aware, you can maintain your effectiveness and happiness.

364

Strive to reduce your program's environmental footprint. Not only does it save money and the planet, but it also feels right. Buy products with limited packaging that last. Recycle everything you can and compost the rest. Plant trees in your backyard and set up vegetable and herb gardens. Switch incandescent light bulbs with compact fluorescent light bulbs and replace inefficient appliances with energy-star rated appliances. Buy energy efficient vehicles and keep them in good shape by regularly changing the oil and maintaining the correct tire pressure. Add weather stripping to doors and caulk around windows. Do whatever you can to make your program as green as possible.

Your residents, staff, and community will appreciate the effort.

365

Be on the side of encouragement and optimism when working with staff and residents.

366

Wear several hats. Let your team know you as a jack of all trades. By mastering many different tasks, you are perceived as a go-to person.

367

Make strong first impressions. Be confident when meeting people. Introduce your program by being approachable, friendly, and fun. If you're not outgoing, this is an important skill to learn. First impressions matter.

368

Abuse and neglect festers where programs are silent. For this reason, make sure that communication is encouraged wherever possible. This is one of the most important reasons I believe in using computer systems. My team can send me a confidential message 24/7 and that can have huge implications.

369

You can get criticized or even sued for what you do as well as what you don't do.

370

Group homes tend to work in the moment with a great deal of trust and freedom to act in the hands of the frontline staff. These conditions can be disastrous for poorly trained and poorly oriented staff. That is why many programs have long training and probationary periods for staff. Staff that are poorly trained often tend to opt for support strategies that are controlling and heavy handed. It is important for group homes to train their staff well and increase their capacity to be more effective.

371

All support interventions must strive to deepen relationships with residents and promote better lifestyles. By being positive and fun, we can usually achieve great results with residents. But not always.

372

The prevalence of trauma with people in care is enormous. As a result, all group homes need to be trauma informed.

373

You have to love working in group homes. If you don't have passion, you will fail. You have to be passionate to persevere. When it gets tough, you have to dig deep and work hard.

374

You have to be a good talent scout. You have to learn how to size people up without knowing them very well and build your organization. You need great support workers to have a good group home. You won't achieve much if your team is untalented and poorly supported.

375

Lead by example. Show your residents patience and respect and try not to be controlling or intolerant. Your team will likely always be closely watching you and one of the most powerful teaching methods is role modelling.

376

Toughen up. As the manager, you will always be the lightening rod of your organization and everybody will tend to blame you first. Accept this reality, and don't let unfair criticism or harshness bruise you.

377

A very skilled and experienced group home operator once told me my best staff will ask for five months leave so they can go sea kayaking in Belize each winter. And she was right. One of the most effective ways to recruit staff is to offer them a great deal of flexibility. I have recruited several staff from highly paid positions to work for me because I offered them lengthy holidays. If you try to recruit on salary alone, you will never build the best team possible because most group homes can't offer comparatively high pay and extensive benefits. However, if you offer a flexible work environment, you will be surprised by the experienced staff you will recruit. Plus, the staff that take lengthy holidays return to work rested and motivated to perform high-caliber work.

378

Most of time the system doesn't get better, but you get better. Concentrate on the things you can affect and let go of the rest.

379

Working in group homes should be your calling. It's hard work, and it's a privilege. Remember that you are working in a group home because you love it. It is what you do and feel lucky to have such an interesting life.

380

So much of the job rests on issues of "wellness." The core responsibility of a group home is to ensure residents are rested, well fed, and receive daily physical activity. If you can achieve these goals on a daily basis, your program will rarely be criticized. Well rested, well nourished residents who engage in daily physical activity are far less likely to have crisis or outburst related behaviors. Every program must take this to heart and promote wellness each and every day.

381

Many staff need less supervision and more vacations.

Maybe cancel your team meetings on occasion and encourage your team to have a paid break instead.

382

IT saves money and time and improves care. It also makes your service more transparent and allows for greater collaboration. But discussing sensitive matters in emails or online poses many security risks and must be approached carefully. In my group homes, we have a communications module that allows us to send emails as well as discuss things openly using a social media feature. All these discussions are behind our firewall where they are secure, private, and monitored. The benefits of using IT are huge and most group homes will benefit from its use.

383

You want to hire staff you totally trust and then get out of there so they can do their job.

384

Many staff need less supervision and more vacations. Maybe cancel your team meetings on occasion and encourage your team to have a paid break instead.

Conclusion

Finally, it all comes down to this: do meaningful work, do work you are proud of, work hard, be smart, and have fun! Your group home needs to be organized but not custodial. You must be open and make decisions on the fly and with authority. While some of these qualities seem contradictory, they really aren't. It's all a question of tone and rapport with your residents and staff.

I once had coffee with a woman who was retiring after a spectacular career working in group homes. She told me that "it all comes down to the people." And by "people" she didn't mean just staff or just residents. Those boundaries had ceased to exist many years earlier for her. We are tasked with the privilege of helping colorful people in a highly personal way. With this opportunity comes a responsibility to apply best practices and ensure the care is as good as it can be. Not the simplest task, but a rich and rewarding career all the same.

www.ingramcontent.com/pod-product-compliance
Lightning Source LLC
Chambersburg PA
CBHW060544100426
42742CB00013B/2449

9 781927 691120